ENDORSEMENTS FOR
MOMENTOUS DECISIONS

Momentous Decisions is a rare kind of finance book—one forged in the fire of personal loss, yet brimming with hope. With unflinching honesty and hard-earned wisdom, it dares to ask what money is really for. This is not just a book about wealth, but about meaning. In a world obsessed with optimization and accumulation, *Momentous Decisions* points the way to a more human, more soulful approach to money—one grounded in values, relationships, and the things that endure. It's a timely guide for anyone seeking clarity, healing, and purpose at the intersection of life and finance.

Dr. Daniel Crosby, *NYT* Bestselling Author of *The Soul of Wealth*

As a career and life coach, I've read countless personal development books—but *Momentous Decisions* truly stands out. From the very first chapter, I could not put it down. Author Brian Muller has crafted something incredibly special: a book that is not only deeply personal and vulnerable but also packed with practical wisdom and real-life application.

Brian's M.A.D.E. Life Framework is a game changer. It's not about doing more—it's about doing what matters most. His insights into wealth, health, and purpose are presented in a way that's both inspiring and achievable, no matter where you are in life. What struck me most was how Brian transforms profound loss into a powerful message of hope and intentionality. This book isn't just about success—it's about living fully and meaningfully.

If you're ready to take bold, momentous steps toward a richer life, this is the guidebook you've been waiting for.

Paula Melo Doroff, Career & Life Coach, Speaker, and Author of *One Decision Away*

"What are you doing to bring joy into your life?" This is a sincere and challenging question Brian Muller asks his readers. My initial response was a big smile and the words, "Reading this amazing book!" It is a captivating, easy-to-read, brilliant LIFE PLAN based on both the personal experiences of Brian and the wisdom of great leaders who preceded him. It will enrich anyone who reads and applies its teachings. You'll learn invaluable life lessons about what successful people do in the most important areas of life. And it will, indeed, bring joy into your life—and the lives of others.

Hal Urban, Author of *Life's Greatest Lessons*

Brian has truly hit the mark with *Momentous Decisions*. We all face the reality that one day our journey will come to an end, and we hope to look back with pride rather than regret. Yet confronting our mortality—and choosing the right path forward—is never easy. Drawing from his own experiences, Brian guides readers through a thoughtful process to uncover what they truly want from life and how to pursue it with purpose. *Momentous Decisions* is both a heartfelt journey and a practical, step-by-step guide to building a life that you—and the people you love—can be proud of.

Alan Moore, CEO of XYPN

Momentous Decisions is an invitation to shift from letting life happen to making life happen. Through his own journey of success and loss, Brian shows that building wealth isn't about following formulas—it's about being intentional with the choices we make every day. It's about understanding what truly matters to us and letting that guide the way.

Brian's M.A.D.E. Life framework isn't just about money—it's about aligning what we do with why we do it. It's about creating the space to live in a way that feels purposeful, and using our resources to reflect that vision. It's not about chasing a number, but about crafting a life with intention.

In a world that often feels chaotic and out of our control, Momentous Decisions provides a refreshing perspective—a reminder that we can choose where to put our energy, where to invest, and what kind of future we want to create.

Stacey Morgenstern, Founder,
Health Coach Institute (acquired) | Keynote Speaker

This book will tug at your heartstrings, spark your motivation, and leave you inspired—with real, actionable steps to start living a better life today. One of the most powerful ways to grow is by learning from the experiences of others, and Brian does just that. Through relatable and heartfelt stories and hard-won wisdom, he shows us how small, momentous decisions can lead to lasting change—and ultimately, the life we've always dreamed of.

Derek N.H. Notman, CFP®, Founder and CEO at Couplr AI,
Co-Founder of REBL Dads

MOMENTOUS DECISIONS

MOMENTOUS DECISIONS

7 STEPS TO BETTER HEALTH, MORE WEALTH, AND A RICHER LIFE

BRIAN D. MULLER

WILEY

Library of Congress Cataloging-in-Publication Data Applied for:

ISBN: 9781394321520 (cloth)
ISBN: 9781394321544 (ePDF)
ISBN: 9781394321537 (ePub)

Cover Design: Paul Mccarthy
Cover Art: © Getty Images | Massimo Colombo

Printed and bound by CPI Group (UK) Ltd, Croydon, CR0 4YY

C9781394321520_120625

To my father:
Who taught me so much about being smart with money.

To my mother:
Who gave me the gift of creativity, music, positivity, and passion.

To my kids:
Who showed me the meaning of life.

To my friends:
Who supported me through the good and bad times.

To Amie:
Your life and legacy will live on and be a part of history. I can only hope to make the impact you did. So many veterans across the United States will be thanking you for many years to come.

To my fiancé Sarah:
I hope to create a richer life with you with more meaning, accomplishments, making a difference and creating amazing experiences. I hope to be the best partner I can be, travel the world with you, and raise life-ready kids.

CONTENTS

CONTENTS

MY STORY

It was April 1988. I was 15 years old and I was three months away from taking my test to get my driver's license. I could almost taste the sweetness of my soon-to-be independence. It was a long cold winter in Minnesota that year with almost 16 consecutive days below freezing in January and with many days below zero in February. I was sitting in my room listening and playing along to Poison's new song "Every Rose Has Its Thorn" on the radio of my four-speaker, two-tweeter Emerson boom box. My dad knew how much I loved music and bought a Mitchell acoustic guitar from a good friend of his a couple years prior. I would play it a little bit. Put it down. Play it. Then put it down, until one day in the early 1990s, I ordered a DVD series called "Play Guitar Overnight." I was always looking for short cuts. I learned best when I just found a song I liked and played along until I got the strumming down. Guitar seemed to come easy for me versus other instruments I tried to master. It wasn't until later in life that I'd realize how important, pivotal, and life changing this day was.

My mom had been in and out of doctors' offices for the past couple weeks and I could tell something was wrong. It was bedtime when my father had gotten home with my mom and I remember him knocking on my door faintly. When he came in, I saw a defeated look on his face as I got up to turn my radio down, which at the time was playing "Devil Inside" by INXS. He sat down on the edge of my brown and tan checkered quilted bedspread that my mom had made with my initials stitched in and said in a shaky voice that there was something he needed to talk to me about. The words that came out of his mouth still ring to this day and forever changed my view on life. On family. He told me that mom had ovarian cancer and the doctor said that she may not live to see her youngest son graduate from high school. My heart felt like it weighed a thousand pounds and I cried so hard my eyes felt like they were going to explode from my head. The thought of not having a mom, the one who nurtured me, was always there for me, just consumed me. In that moment I was numb. I got up off my bed and walked across the hall to see my mom sitting on the edge of her bed. The mascara was running down her face and she looked as though she had seen a ghost. I sat down beside her and held her stronger than I had ever held someone. I said in a whimpering voice as I sucked the snot up my nose repeatedly, "I need you to tell me you're going to fight this. I need you here. I don't know what I will do without you."

That night I stayed up and I couldn't stop crying. I wrote one of my first songs. It was called "That Day." That was the night that changed my view on life and the night I fell in love with songwriting. From that day on I never stopped writing. I'd write whenever I needed it. It got me through breakups, failures, struggles, and helped me understand a little more about life. It was my outlet. My mom also found her outlet to deal with the long road of cancer treatment. She turned to watercolor painting and poetry to keep her mind positive. I remember picking her up from the hospital after her fourth chemotherapy treatment with my first car. It was a Red Ford Maverick with a black vinyl roof my grandma had given me for getting my license. My mom was very sick by this time, was losing her hair and needed a wheelchair to get from her room to the front of the hospital. I still remember the song "Devil Inside" playing when my dad knocked on my room that night and all I can remember is thinking there is a devil inside my mom just slowly killing her from the inside.

She was so frail and weak and spent a lot of time in the bathroom when we got home.

Over the coming year my mom fought cancer head-on with a positivity and strength I had only seen in the movies. The one thing I learned from my mom is that if you're going to beat something like cancer, you're going to have to beat it with your mind as well as the power of medicine. She prayed, she wrote poems, she painted. She did everything she could to stay positive and stay strong. After a year of fighting cancer, countless treatments of chemotherapy, and losing all of her hair, she proved that doctor wrong and was there to see me graduate from high school in 1992. And college. And despite another fight with cancer 10 years later she has been there to see me buy my first home, get married, and bear witness to four grandchildren between my brother and me.

During my college years I studied finance and economics and was the president of the St. Cloud State Investment Club. I spent a lot of my free time writing songs about life, searching, wanting more, and heartbreak. I remember coming home from beer and bagel night at a bar called D.B. Searls and climbing out onto my roof and playing my guitar to the people in the alley walking by. They weren't always the best audience, most of them drunk and telling me to shut the f-up. Writing and singing was my passion but thanks to my dad, I also had a passion for the stock market. I loved researching stocks and following the markets. I was fortunate to know what I wanted to do right out of college. I wanted to be a financial advisor, or back then they were mostly referred to as stockbrokers. My roommates would always make fun of me because I'd be watching CNBC after class when they clearly wanted to be playing Sega NHL 95 on the living room TV that was on top of an entertainment center made out of Busch Light bottle boxes.

After graduating from SCSU in 1996, I bought some fancy shoes, some nice silk striped ties, and some skinny leather suspenders, and I got a job at a full-service discount stockbrokerage firm, which seemed like an oxymoron but they hired me so I was grateful for the opportunity. My job was to cold call out of the phone book and when I got a good lead who wanted more information on our special commission free account, I had to give that lead to a senior broker. I think my pay was $1500 per month plus commissions. Just enough for some beer money after all the bills were paid. After about nine months of getting beaten up on the phone and watching my senior broker rake in the dough while I continued to get my near poverty-level paycheck, I started to look for a better option where all my efforts would benefit me.

I interviewed with a major brokerage firm with the most intimidating man. He had a fierce stare that gleamed over the glasses near the tip of his nose. He asked me if I would hire myself and why? Tough question I thought. My answer, "I would hire myself in a heartbeat because I have a desire to succeed and a drive to help as many people make sense of investing as I can."

That started my journey in the investment business. When times got tough, I turned to music. I wrote hundreds of songs relating to the ups and downs of the markets and life in general. Without music, I am not sure I would have made it through the bear market from 2000 to 2002 or the financial crisis of 2008–2009.

Here I am today, after 24+ years as a financial advisor, a dad to three kids, three albums with the Brian David Band, seven singles as a solo artist, and many more songs waiting to be written. I have had my share of ups and downs, disappointments, failures, and successes. The difference is that most of my life is documented through dusty boxes of half-written songs, lyrics, and feelings. After digging through my archive of all my lyrics I have written over the years, I realized there is a message in my music. I don't necessarily write all uplifting motivational songs, but there is insight and perspective in each one. Lessons I hope people can relate to and maybe learn something from. The last album I recorded with the band was called "There From Here" and became part of the inspiration for this book. You can see the lyrics and get links to many of the songs I have written over the years in Appendix 4 of this book.

Many authors of personal growth books ask the question, "What would you do if you found out you had six months to live?" I got to live that question, except it wasn't me, it was my wife Amie, and there was nothing I could do about it, except live it with her. That diagnosis for my wife forever changed my life. My only regret is not going into the darkness with her. I just couldn't. I couldn't accept that a 36-year-old woman and the mother of my children could not beat cancer, even though it was one of the worst kinds.

I think a better question than what would you do if you had six months to live, is "What are you going to do right now to make the time you have left count?" Are you going to dwell on the past? Focus too much on the future? Or live each day with more purpose. With more meaning.

I never thought in a million years that the song I wrote when I was 15 called "That Day" would repeat itself nearly 30 years later when my wife, Amie, was diagnosed with pancreatic cancer in 2016.

"That Day" that I had when I was 15 and again when I was 44, can happen to anyone. It could be later today or tomorrow and for many of you reading this book, it has already happened. But you have a choice. You can either let "That Day" define you or that day remind you. If you let it define you, you become trapped in its power to suck you in and keep you stuck. Or you can let it remind you of what is important truly in life. Let it remind you to love deeply. Let it remind you to be open and selfless. Let it remind you that you are stronger than you think. You will be defined or you will defy.

We have all heard the expression, "You never know how strong you are until being strong is the only choice you have." That was my mom. That was my wife. You find strength when you need it. No matter how much pain comes into your life, there is always something inside you that is stronger than pain. There is always something greater to hold onto. Or the expression "God gives you only what you can handle." This one can be hard to believe because everyone in their lifetime is going to be given a situation that seems more than they could ever handle. If we are prepared emotionally, physically, and spiritually then we can handle anything. But if you're not, the circumstances of life will feel much more than you can handle.

No experience exists in life that does not have the power to lead you to greater knowledge and growth. Trust in your ability to figure things out. You can take "That Day" and have it shape you. Shape you into a stronger you. A stronger you that can take on any challenge. You can walk through any darkness to the light. You can choose to go through something or you can choose to grow through something.

AMIE'S STORY

My wife, Amie, a two-time Iraq War Veteran, was diagnosed with Stage III pancreatic cancer in April 2016, two weeks after her thirty-sixth birthday. After an eight-month battle, we found out the cancer had spread to her liver. Surgery was off the table and everything went downhill from there. We celebrated Thanksgiving and Christmas like it was our last. In the beginning of February 2017, what was supposed to be a procedure called a celiac block turned into complication after complication. The two-hour-long car ride to the Mayo Clinic along with being off her blood thinners for 24 hours caused a blood clot in her leg. The focus turned from relieving her pain to getting this blood clot under control. Her liver scores were bad, her skin yellow with jaundice, her pain at an 11 out of 10. We spent three weeks at the Methodist Hospital hoping to get Amie home, but it never happened. The day after Valentine's Day something awful happened. It was the first night I had spent away from the hospital in five days. Carole, Amie's mom, texted me to come to the hospital right away. When I got there, Amie was trying to talk, but nothing was coming out right. Every word was mumbled. I will never forget the look on Amie's face that morning. She knew something had happened and that we couldn't understand her. It was the worst day of my life. Seeing the fear in the love of your life's eyes. Wanting to know what she was trying to say and knowing you will never be able to communicate with your wife again. That was the day everything turned and became much more real. I didn't want to believe before that things were progressing this fast. A week prior the oncologist told us we had maybe three months. Two days prior, we were told weeks and now it appeared like we might have days. The doctor came in later to tell us that Amie most likely had a minor stroke during the night. Three days later, surrounded by close family and friends, Amie took her last breath. It was peaceful but labored and stressful with each breath. Every breath felt like it was going to be her last. I know she didn't want to go. She fought so hard and with a courage I will always greatly admire. They say that hearing is the last to go and I know she could hear us in those final minutes. When she took her last breath, her bottom lip turned down and made what appeared to be a frown and a single yellow tear showed up in the corner of each eye. She knew she was leaving us. She knew it was her last breath. Those last minutes will forever be cemented in my mind. It will be hard to ever get over the hurt, but my commitment to her is to go on. To go on and make a difference. Make a difference in people's lives. Make a difference in pancreatic cancer research. Make a difference in the awareness of illnesses resulting from veterans being exposed to the toxic "burn pits" in Iraq and Afghanistan.

Amie's fight was the hardest thing I have ever been through. We both wanted more for our lives and had big dreams together. Now, I have to find a way to pursue those dreams without her. The only thing that has gotten me through this is my kids, my family and friends, writing songs, personal growth, meditation, and journalling. Most of my life is documented through dusty boxes of half-written songs, lyrics, and feelings, but this was different. I wrote over 50 songs about grief and loss during the first six months after Amie passed away, most of which will never be sung or played again.

Reevaluating Life and What is Important

One thing the horrible experience of losing the mother of my children did was cause me to reevaluate my life. I looked through old notebooks and found a common theme. I knew I wanted more (over half of the songs I have written had that theme) and I knew I had more in me, but always seemed to fall short of my own expectations when it came to reaching my goals and life aspirations. Long before Amie's cancer fight, I knew I had to find answers rather than just writing about my problems and what I thought I was lacking. I started reading personal growth and self-development books that were recommended by Oprah or someone I respected about 14 years ago and continued to read them on and off during Amie's fight, to try and remain positive. It started with a book called *Who Moved My Cheese* by Spencer Johnson. This book was so simple and such a great story and made me realize through its simple message that the biggest inhibitor to change lies within yourself, and that nothing gets better until you change. It gave me a newfound respect for fear and the fact that it is irrational most of the time and can keep you from action. It also made me realize that change was the only way I was going to find a better life. A better cheese. This was the start of my personal growth and self-development journey. Then came books like *The Last Lecture* by Randy Pausch, *The Secret* by Rhonda Byrne, *Tuesdays with Morrie* by Mitch Albom, *Man's Search for Meaning* by Viktor Frankl, *The 5 People You Meet In Heaven* by Mitch Albom, and *The Power of Intentions* by the late Dr. Wayne Dyer. This was the meaning phase of my journey, which eventually led into books more focused on personal growth, sales, influence, how to deal with people, attitude, positivity, drive, motivation, ambition, habit, productivity, mindfulness, finance, learned optimism, and success. (For a complete list of the 100+ books I have read over the last 10 years go to the end of this book.) So what happened that sparked the obsession?

Frankly I had hit a wall. I was letting my past define me and mediocrity set in. I was successful by most standards, making a good living, had a nice home in a sought-after neighborhood, had a good business and good friends, a growing family, but I wasn't feeling completely fulfilled. I wasn't feeling like I was coming anywhere near my potential. I was letting comfort be the enemy of my achievement and I was letting myself be somewhat content with where I was at. So I started digging for answers and started finding them one by one with each book. I committed to reading one book every two weeks by waking up early at 5 a.m. When you have two little ones under the age of five and a teenager who needs to be woken up at 6 a.m. to get ready for school, this is the only time that you can truly have for you.

Here I am today, finally in a position to reach my full potential. I own my own financial planning and wealth management firm called Momentous Wealth Advisors, I have a podcast called "Wealth Decisions by Brian" I do each week to educate people on crucial wealth decisions, and I have big aspirations to launch The Momentous Wealth Academy to teach teens and young adults important wealth and financial habits. I am in the best shape of my life at age 51 and live an active lifestyle of playing pickleball two or three times per week and H.I.I.T. training two or three times per week. I finally feel like I am living my purpose. I feel more alive and excited about the future than I ever have. I owe that to my past but also to the compelling vision I have created of the future and what I want my life to stand for.

I believe we all want to live a richer life. That is what we are all here for: to grow, learn, and live life to the fullest, to become better human beings, and to strive for excellence in all areas of life. *Momentous Decisions: 7 Steps to Better Health, More Wealth, and a Richer Life* is a book for anyone who wants a permanent change in their health habits, wealth habits, and their most important relationships. It's a framework for designing a better life for you and your family. New habits form because of the decisions you make each day and eventually become part of who you are. These momentous decisions take hold only if you change how you view yourself, how you view your health, how you view your financial situation, and how you view your relationships. This book is structured in a way to help you change your mindset and beliefs to create lasting change and give you crucial life, wealth, and health decisions to implement to create better health, more wealth, and a richer life. One year from now, three years from now, and 10 years from now, you will be able to look back at this decision you made today to improve your life.

MO■MEN■TOUS

(of a decision, event, or change) of great importance or significance, especially in its bearing on the future.

First off, if you have a family that loves you, a roof over your head, and strong friendships you are already living a rich life. But I believe life can be richer for all of us. To live a richer life, many important decisions need to be made about your health, life, and financial habits. A life with wealth but poor health is not a richer life. Excellent health, but no financial security or plan is promising. However, it won't allow you to do all the things you want in life, whether that is achieving financial freedom, traveling the world, or leaving a legacy. Being healthy and wealthy with no deep-quality relationships is also not a rich life. A richer life is about finding a balance of all the things that bring life meaning. It's about accomplishing things without sacrificing your most important relationships. It's about making a difference in the lives of others. It's about experiencing all that life has to offer.

We have three choices:

1. We can be proactive with our decisions because we want to live a better life.
2. We can be reactive with our decisions because we have to, because of a health scare, because our marriage is falling apart, or a reality check of where we are financially.
3. We can choose to be defined by our circumstances and not make the decisions necessary to change our lives, our health, or our financial situation.

The first choice is what I think is the best option. Let's be honest though. It is hard to be proactive. Most of us are reactive. My goal is to help you create a proactive plan to build your wealth, become healthier, and have more fulfillment and meaning in your life. It has been said that the circumstances of life reveal you. It is sometimes hard to have faith in yourself, but when you are growing in life and improving each day, the faith you build in yourself will remind you of who you are and who you are becoming.

THE BIG LIFE QUESTION

Do we have a life plan, a predestined path?

Some people believe we have a predestined path. Just know that everything you do at this very instant is what matters. You cannot change your destination overnight, but you can change your direction. So, the bigger life question is: How do you want to be remembered? To your loved ones? To others? If you were out of your body in the audience of your life celebration, what would you want to hear? What would you want your life to stand for?

Looking back at your life, what have you made of it? In this book, I explore in depth a framework I developed for life that I call the M.A.D.E. Life Philosophy. I developed this framework after my wife Amie died in 2017, as a guide to live a better life. I don't have all the answers, and I certainly don't have a perfect life. There are many things in the accomplishment category I had to dial back on because of being a single dad raising kids on my own. I still have big goals and things I want to accomplish, but they are just different. They are less about success and reaching the next level of income and more about fulfillment and purpose. I remember hearing a quote, "the life you lead is the lesson you teach." So, what life do you want to live? One that makes you proud? One that is remembered? One that makes an impact in the lives of those you care about?

Here is the M.A.D.E. Life framework:

M– Meaning – What had meaning?

A–Accomplish – What did you accomplish?

D– Difference – What difference did you make in the life of your family and others?

E–Experiences – What experiences do you want to have now and in the future?

The M.A.D.E. Life framework is centered around a philosophy of the following eight principles:

1. Experiences are more important than things.
2. Strong relationships should be centered around the three As: attention, affection, and appreciation.
3. Your health is paramount to being able to enjoy your wealth.
4. Having a financial plan can contribute to your overall well-being.

5. Living with intention leads to more fulfillment and joy.
6. Giving back is a priceless life experience.
7. Comfort is the enemy of achievement.
8. Your why behind your why is what will keep you inspired long-term.

This book is laid out in a way that gives you all the tools to help you transform your health, wealth, and life. Before you can change your life for the better, you first need to understand how to transform your habits into lasting change that become new standards, which I discuss in detail in Chapter 1. Next, you need to discover what things have been getting in your way, preventing you from creating better health and wealth habits, which I discuss in Chapter 2. In Chapter 3, you will use a framework for designing your ideal life and start envisioning what you want your rich life to look like. In Chapters 4–8, I discuss some of the most important life, wealth, and health decisions to help you start building a life with a new set of principles to guide you in developing your version of a richer life. The M.A.D.E. Life Framework will be used to create a 90-day plan to improve your health, your wealth, and the balance in your life, which you will find in the final 7 Steps chapter of this book.

We don't have to have all the answers right now. All we can do is live our lives each day with gratitude and intention and without noticing; one day, we will live into the answers. We can make better decisions to shape a better now and build a stronger future.

One of the toughest battles you will ever face is the battle in your head – the battle between your old view and a new you.

Old View vs. New You

If you want things to be the same, keep thinking the same things. If you want things to be different, it's time to set aside your old views and make room for the new you.

Old View:	Life happens to me
New You:	I control the direction of my life
Old View:	Bad things happen
New You:	I control how I respond
Old View:	I have past limiting beliefs that are holding me back
New You:	Limitations and lack are made up.
Old View:	I used to not believe in myself
New You:	I can change my belief at any moment
Old View:	I cannot find joy
New You:	Joy can be found at any time
Old View:	My past is baggage keeping me stuck
New You:	My story can be rewritten
Old View:	I wished I had more
New You:	I am grateful every day for what I have
Old View:	I have dwelled on my mistakes
New You:	I highlight my triumphs and wins
Old View:	I used to say "I have to"
New You:	Now I stay "I get to"
Old View:	I used to dread getting up
New You:	I wake up expecting good things
Old View:	I used to get down when something bad happened
New You:	Bad things can lead to something better
Old View:	My health and fitness took the back seat
New You:	I am in the process of taking good care of myself

Your old views are done! The new you starts today. We all live two lives: the one we live now and the one we are capable of. Never settle for anything less than you are capable of.

INTRODUCTION

SETTING THE STAGE
FOR A RICHER LIFE

So, what does a richer life mean to you? Everyone has a different definition of what a rich life means, and it is not just about wealth, money, or success. A rich life, to me, is about finding purpose, meaning, and fulfillment in all areas of our lives. It is about living with intention, driven by our values and what is most important to us.

As adults, we may have gotten lost in thinking that more success and things will create more happiness. If we get that new boat, it will make us happier. If we buy a bigger house, that will make us happy. We are a work in progress, and I include myself. I was always very driven most of my life, and I am sure I always will be, but what I have found through reflection after my wife, Amie, died in 2017 is that it is okay to set aside some ambition if it is not aligning with your goals of living a more balanced, richer life. If ambition is robbing you of joy, then it is okay to take a step back and reevaluate what is more important. Nobody on their deathbed said they wished they had worked more. If your health is taking a back seat to your aspirations, then pause and make health a priority. If you are grinding every day to make a living, but you are not paying yourself first and investing for the future, then you need to make wealth-building a priority.

If you are working 10–12 hours a day at the expense of your most important relationships, then you need to find more balance and focus some time cultivating deeper relationships.

For the first year, as I dealt with the loss of my wife and the mother of my children, I did everything I possibly could to deal with my grief. I journaled. I did therapy. I meditated. I wrote over 40 songs on grief and loss. I exercised. I read books on grief, loss, and resilience. I poured my pain into purpose and started a foundation to help veterans who were also exposed to Burn Pits and had pancreatic cancer, only to find that although it felt great to offer help, I was also reliving my wife's fight over and over again. Even though it was very fulfilling and gave me purpose, it prevented me from finding joy and possibly moving on to live this richer life I felt obligated to live. I still wanted to continue helping families and raising awareness about the harmful effects of the Burn Pits our veterans were exposed to in Iraq and Afghanistan, but I had to find a way to bring joy to my life again. One of the things that brings joy to me is music and kids. So, we got the Brian David Band back together, reached out to some old musician friends, and started doing a live music event each year to raise money for the Amie Muller Foundation. Practicing and rehearsing for this show was a highlight of each year for me. It brought me back to why I loved music in the first place. Being on stage and singing my heart out always brought so much joy, and I had forgotten how important that was to me. Then, the board of the Amie Muller Foundation brainstormed ideas for doing a family fun event to raise money. We started doing a Family Fun Day at the Mall of America each year, with fun auction items, cartoon mascots, balloon art, and magicians. These two events gave me something to look forward to. They gave me purpose but also joy.

Before Amie died, a good friend came to visit and had her write down some things she wanted for me and the kids. These notes became one of the most sentimental things she left behind, and I made a graphic of them and called them Amie's Rules for Life.

Amie's Rules for Life:

1. Pursue Your Dreams
2. Love Deeply
3. Always Be Kind
4. Have a Pet
5. Follow Your Heart
6. Have a Passion
7. Read Often
8. Camp and Sleep Under the Stars

I put a lot of pressure on myself to try to live life to the fullest after Amie died. Probably too much pressure. I tried to make everything extra special for the kids. I went all out for Christmas and Halloween. I bought a 20-foot Coleman trailer, and we started camping at all the best campgrounds in Minnesota and even took a two-week camping road trip to the Black Hills, Devil's Tower, and Colorado. I will never forget those trips. They are forever burned in my mind and were a form of therapy being in nature and creating these amazing experiences for my kids.

I knew I needed to bring a passion back into my life again, so I started writing music again and eventually put out eight singles from 2021 to 2023. I kept reading self-development books to stay positive, and in February 2024, I pursued my dream of having my own financial planning and wealth management firm and starting a podcast. Today I am the founder of Momentous Wealth Advisors and do a weekly podcast called Wealth Decisions by Brian.

You don't need a traumatic event to happen in your life to change things for the better. You just need to decide right now that you want something more. If you are reading this book, you have already decided you want more for your life. I want to congratulate you for taking that first step. The fact that you know there are things you want to improve or change and are willing to work on them is a giant leap from where most people are. Accepting that things need to change or that you can improve is half the battle. The answers and motivation you need to transform your life may not just come into your life at one point but in parts. I hope to give you a spark to think and reflect on what is most important to you at this point in your life. Decide what you truly want your life to look like in the next 5–10 years and beyond. The past has little to do with your future unless you let it. If you read this book in its entirety and take action by setting new standards for yourself, create a new vision for your life, and take the time to craft a M.A.D.E. LifePlan, you will be on your way to living a richer life. But things won't change unless you take action. Not all at once, but small actions every day. The M.A.D.E. 90-Day LifePlan is about making one commitment in each area of the M.A.D.E. framework every 90 days. It's about taking small steps toward a richer, more balanced life.

What Stops Us from Changing Our Life?

What stops most of us changing our life? Fear? Lack of confidence? The past? Worry? Stress? Or is it just a lack of time? A lot of people don't take action because they fear that it might just be a waste of their time. If they change their habits and put forth the effort that they need to, they won't get the results that they are looking to achieve. Nobody wants to waste their time. Nobody wants to put forth more effort with fewer results. The key is not giving up at the first sign of failure. You will have a period of time where you still feel like you are going sideways with more effort, and then all of a sudden, six months from now, one year from now, 18 months from now, things start compounding. Your health will improve, your net worth will start to grow in the right direction, and your relationships will improve.

Always Try to Do Your Best

Bring your best self to each day. If you don't do your best each day, you will have regrets down the road. You will look back, thinking you could have done better.

I have wasted my fair share of time in my life coasting along with no measurable progress, and I can tell you from experience that it doesn't feel good in the future. Jim Rohn often said, "We must all suffer one of two things: the pain of discipline or the pain of regret." It's your choice. He goes on to say that the pain of discipline weighs ounces, but the pain of regret weighs tons. If you don't choose discipline, you automatically get the pain of regret.

There will be ups and downs and moments when you go sideways. My first single as a solo artist in 2006 was titled "Up Down Sideways" and became the theme for my life at that time. We have all had ups and downs in our lives. We have all had those weeks, months, or even years when we felt like we went nowhere or didn't make progress. That's okay. The past is the past. Learn from those times. It's part of life to have ups and downs, and you will not always have success after success without some failure along the way. You will have lows, then see the light. You will feel wrong, then feel right. Believe in your ability to choose the thoughts to get you through, take the action to find your way, and learn the things to get you back on the right path toward the life you envision for yourself. You will fall. You will falter. But in the end you will be better. To quote a line from my song "There From Here," "When the inches turn into feet, and the feet become yards, without ever knowing defeat, you will never know who you really are."

I remember a point in my life when I was drifting. I was making an average living and pursuing my dreams of being a singer/songwriter/rock star. Every song I wrote during that period was, well, kind of a downer. I would always make the excuse that most songwriters say in interviews: "I write sad songs because those end up being the best songs that come from a place of hurt and heartbreak." I would write songs that weren't necessarily uplifting to get them off my chest and go on with my life being happy. Well, I wasn't completely happy because, by focusing so much on music, I was neglecting my talent and potential as a financial advisor. The regret of knowing that I could have done better started to paralyze me, and it was tough to find that spark again when I would see my friends getting ahead while I was falling further and further behind. Of course, I was only falling behind financially in terms of my income goals or the ones that were set for me by the firm I was at during that time. I was having a blast performing and recording music. Most people dream of being on a stage and wish they could do some of the things I have done, and that's what I held on to. I went for it. I gave it my all and have no regrets. Sometimes you just have to follow your heart. And that is where my heart was at that point in time.

Deciding What You Truly Want

Deciding what you truly want is the first step to live a richer life. Where do you want to go? Where do you want to be? What do you want most for you and your family? I have written hundreds of songs about not being where I want to be – wanting more. I have read my share of self-help books, but I didn't do anything to change. I guess I always had an excuse, one I convinced myself was valid. Or maybe I didn't connect with what the author was trying to say. Or maybe it was too intense, too methodical or psychological. Or maybe it just seemed too hard. There were too many worksheets or questions to answer when the answers just lay within.

Making a positive change starts within. It starts with a spark that ignites something in you. Some of the things in this book might be common sense or things you may have heard before, but as we know, common sense is not necessarily common practice. It's been said that each day something new comes into your life or something new comes out of you. I hope to bring something new into your life but also, in the end, bring something new out of you. There is a deeper level of change in you. Ask yourself why you are not where you would like to be. What is in your way? What are the obstacles? What are the habits that need to change? Without the old you in the way. So, what do you truly want? This is the first step of the 7 Steps to Better Health, More Wealth, and a Richer Life, and we will dig into it later in this book.

At the End of the Old, Start Your New Beginning

To quote Dan Wilson's band Semisonic, "Every new beginning comes from some other beginning's end." Make this day the day you start your new beginning. A new life that is more fulfilling, present, engaging, and purposeful. To start your new beginning, look at everything you have done to get where you are. Be proud of your success, but understand there is more in you. Brian Tracy talks about starting at the beginning by doing what he calls zero-based thinking. He says, "In zero-based thinking, you ask this question, 'Knowing what I now know, is there anything that I am doing today that I wouldn't start up again today if I had to do it over, knowing what I now know?'" Evaluate every part of your life and be prepared to make the changes needed. Start fresh with a new perspective. Imagine your future is exactly how you want it. What would have to happen to make that future a reality? Living a richer life starts today by creating a new vision for your life. I will discuss how to create a strong vision for your life in the 7 Steps chapter.

Your Turning Point Starts Now

You've lacked direction. You've missed some turns. What's around the corner on your new path? Mark this day as your "Turning Point." The day you didn't just round the corner but turned your life 180 degrees and found a new direction. This chapter of your life is done, and a new one has begun. It might be hard to see at the moment; it might be hard to know. The path to take is going to be new for you. There will be new challenges along the way. Along the journey you will start to feel a greater sense of fulfillment – a greater sense of purpose. They say your life will only get better when you get better. We know from all the best self-help authors that there are no limits on how much better you can become and no limits on how grand your life can become. Your decision to be better today has the ability to be that turning point in your life. It starts now. With one decision. To be better.

Getting Rid of the Vagueness in Your Goals

We have all had vague goals before in our life. A vague goal is thought about and usually not acted upon because, well, it is not specific. There is no way to measure the progress because there is no end destination. We have all heard the expression, "You get what you ask for." If we are vague, we will end up with vague results. Getting specific about what we want isn't always easy, but it is necessary if we want to live a richer life.

Seeing Past the Sea of Excuses

"In the shadows they hide, all the voices that tempt you, trying to keep you behind in the dark of the blue, In the glimmers of hope, there's room to believe past excuses you've made into a great big sea."

– "The Next Mile," Brian David Band

We have all made our share of excuses. Some of us could fill a sea with them. Anyone can get what they want in life if they just rid their life of debilitating thoughts. You are responsible for how your song plays. We can always keep close a reason for not having something more in our lives. We are good at selling ourselves a reason we are not further along. We can be really convincing. Maybe we think we should play it safe or be more of a realist, or maybe we convince ourselves that we really don't want what we are trying to achieve. Fear of the unknown can be very scary for most of us, so we stay where we are. We know what to expect. One year from now, five years from now, ten years from now you will know the benefits of a better life, and you will look back and say, "I am so glad I stopped making excuses and took action." Stop using excuses like, "I'm too busy," "I'll do it someday," "It's too late for me now," "I don't know where to start," "It won't pan out the way I would want." Make the time, don't delay, and believe that you deserve a richer life.

Are You Running from Failures, or Learning from Them

We all have had failures. Sometimes we face them head-on, and sometimes we run from them. How do we overcome them? We need to use each failure as a stepping stone. As opportunities to learn and grow.

I remember when I was laid off from a sales job. I went into a deep state of depression and lost my confidence. I sold my nice car and traded it in for a vehicle with no power windows or locks, thinking that I was never going to find success again. I let that event get the best of me until I woke up one day and realized that I had success before that job. I started reading positive motivational books and listened to guys like Brian Tracey, Jim Rohn, Dr. Wayne Dyer, and Tony Robbins and got my mojo back. I overwhelmed my failure with positivity so it got buried in a vault of my triumphs. We have so much personal power in us we can overcome anything. Some say that circumstances are almost made to bring out the best in us or see what we are made of.

Never Stop Trying

It was the spring of 2008, and we were in the final round of a battle of the bands competition that would, if we won, give us an opening slot at a summer music festival called the Basilica Block Party. We had the fan base, the songs, and a set list we rehearsed that flowed smoothly from one song to the next, like an '80s rock concert. We played our hearts out that night, thinking that if we moved the crowd, we would prevail. We had a set list well rehearsed, and about three-quarters of the fans in the crowd were there for us. I sang my heart out that night, as evidenced by my sweat-covered T-shirt that could be wrung out to fill an eight-ounce glass. I engaged with the crowd, hit every note, and put every ounce of energy into every song.

After the competing bands finished their sets, they announced the winner and the band that would be playing at this year's Basilica Block Party. We anxiously waited, hanging on every reverb-enhanced word from the announcer's mouth. It was almost like it was in slow motion. The words that rolled out were not ours. There was a state of shock in the room for a brief second, and then some faint claps for the other band. My heart sank. We had put so much into this battle, and it hit me like a ton of heavy Gibson guitars. I looked at my bandmates in disbelief. Our fans came up to us with a look quite the same. We did our best and put on a great show, but it wasn't our time.

That night, when I got home, I penned the song that would eventually be the title track of our album "There From Here." The first line in the song says it all: "I've had my share of triumphs, just enough to keep trying." This event started a spark in me to keep trying to reach my goals with music. It ignited a charge in me to improve, write better songs, and improve my performance. Less than a year later, we finished the album "There From Here" and played to a 400+ crowd at the Fine Line Music Cafe in Minneapolis. It was a night I will never forget and thanks to Amie and her team of photographers and videographers, we have the whole night documented. Who would have thought the album and its content would inspire me to write this book 15 years later? I hope you will find inspiration in the content in this book that will help ignite an internal drive to help you on your journey of transformation. Everything you want in life is before you; it's just on the other side of a decision.

The Facts of Life

I remember reading Steve Jobs' "Five Undeniable Facts of Life," and I often go back to those and reread them every once in a while just to check in on some of my standards and values I have set for being a father, a partner, and a quality human being.

Steve Jobs' Five Undeniable Facts of Life:

- Number one, don't educate your children to be rich. Educate them to be happy. So when they grow up, they will know the value of things and not the price.
- Number two, best-awarded words in London, eat your food as your medicines. Otherwise, you have to eat medicines as your food.
- Number three, the one who loves you will never leave you for another because even if there are a hundred reasons to give up, he or she will find the one reason to hold on.
- Number four, there's a big difference between being a human being and being human. Only a few really understand it.
- And number five, you are loved when you are born. You'll be loved when you die. In between, you have to manage.

Steve Jobs also said the six best doctors in the world are sunlight, rest, exercise, diet, self-confidence, and friends. Maintain them at all stages of life, and you'll enjoy a really healthy, rich life.

Finding Purpose

When I was 12 years old, I used to sit in the park by the lake, watch the sunset by myself, and think about life. Who does that when they are 12? Not sure what I really thought about, but it was the beginning of my quest to find purpose in my life. What is your life for? Why are you here? Is what you're doing right now all for you, or do you think there is more? We are all destined for bigger things. One of the songs I am most proud of that I put out in 2021 was a song inspired by a church sermon at Crossroads Church in Woodbury. It was called "What On Earth." The first verse of the song is, "There's a pebble in your shoe, you know what to do, but you don't shake it out, like all of your doubts. Once you taste it, you'll never go back, so don't you waste it, slip through the cracks, do you wonder if there's more?" I believe there is more for you. I believe there is more for me. You just have to take the pebble out of your shoe and get rid of your doubts. Once you get a taste of what life can be, you will never go back.

See what can be, not just what is. When you truly believe you can do more, your mind expands and shows you the way. This journey is yours to own. What will your moment be?

Finding Your Moment

I believe there will be three big moments that will start to change your life:

Moment #1: The day you change your belief and mindset on what is possible for you.

Moment #2: The day you act on that new belief and start to make progress.

Moment #3: The day you create an internal inspiration that pulls you toward living your best life.

What I hope this book will do is create those moments for you. I hope to help you change your self-image so you can create lasting change. I hope to give you a new vision for your life by inspiring you to think about what you truly want and create a plan to live a better life. I hope to make you feel good about what you have done so far and inspire you to think bigger. I hope to help you change your habits into new standards so that you become a new version of yourself. I hope to help you live a healthier, wealthier, richer life.

CHAPTER ONE

TRANSFORMING YOUR SELF-IMAGE: THE KEY TO LASTING HEALTH AND WEALTH HABITS

T he first three chapters of this book will help you understand how to create lasting change, get rid of the obstacles that have been in your way, and help you get clarity on what you want your new life to be like in the future. You can't create a plan without understanding why things possibly haven't improved in the past. You can't develop a richer life without defining what a rich life means to you. The key to having better health, creating more wealth, and living a richer life is not a new fad diet or get-rich schemes; it is about creating strong habits that become new standards. It starts with transforming your self-image. You need to see yourself as a healthier person, someone who has strong wealth habits and deserving

15

of a better life. Of course, you can't just visualize this healthier or wealthier person and the pounds will melt off, or money will fall out of trees, but if you don't transform your self-image, you won't create lasting health habits, and you won't do the things you need to do consistently to build and keep your wealth over time. The fundamental truth is your habits are a reflection of your identity. When we try to change our behavior without addressing our underlying beliefs and identity, we set ourselves up for failure.

When it comes to achieving significant health or financial goals, many people focus just on behaviors – eat less, exercise more, spend less, and save more. These actions are important, but they don't consider a fundamental principle of creating lasting change: identity.

Your identity – how you see yourself and your beliefs about who you are – shapes your choices and actions more powerfully than using something like willpower. Willpower is not enough. Willpower is like a cell phone battery. It fades and has to be constantly recharged. To create sustainable change you have to shift your identity to align with your goals. No, you don't have to dye your hair, change your name, and get a new license, although many of us wouldn't mind a new picture on our last state license or passport. You have to see yourself differently and attach that new identity with goals and a plan to reach those goals.

Consider two people trying to improve their fitness. Joe thinks, "I'm trying to exercise more," while Mark believes, "I am a health-conscious person." Who do you think is more likely to wake up for early morning workouts consistently? Mark's identity as a health-conscious person leads to choices and behaviors that support that self-image. Now, you don't have to have the identity of an athlete to improve your health and fitness. I play pickleball three or four days per week, and in my mind, I still think I am 35, but this 51-year-old body says differently the next day. Thank god for the 42-degree cold plunge pool at Chip's Pickleball Club. You just have to reframe your beliefs about yourself and commit to having a health-conscious mindset.

The same principle applies to financial goals. Someone who sees themselves as "bad with money" will struggle to maintain good financial habits, while a person who identifies as a savvy investor or a good saver will more easily make choices that grow their wealth.

I remember being roped into watching the show *The Biggest Loser*. If you don't remember that show, it was where contestants competed to see who could lose the most weight. Seeing the agony these contestants went through each week was hard to watch, but also very inspiring. They had personal trainers who worked them to exhaustion every day. I remember some contestants throwing up or fainting. I remember many of them suffering through eating healthy every day when they were used to eating fast food, but in the end, they lost the weight, and some lost enough weight to be crowned "The Biggest Loser." The problem was that the majority of them gained all the weight back after the show was done. They may have worked hard and proved to themselves that they could do it, but they didn't change their identity and how they viewed themselves and they went back to their old health habits.

So, how can you shift your identity to support your health or financial goals?

1. **Envision your ideal self:** Clearly imagine the person you want to become. What does the healthiest or most financially successful version of you believe, do, and value? A healthy person exercises right away in the morning, eats a healthy breakfast, doesn't indulge in fast food, and always carries a water bottle. A healthy person does something active every day, whether that is going for a walk, a bike ride, or playing pickleball. A wealthy person pays themself first, lives within their means, and invests money when it is available for the long term. Wealthy people study the markets, research things before investing, and have a comprehensive financial plan. A wealthy person doesn't speculate; they invest in quality investments

17

with a long-term perspective. A wealthy person knows where their money is going and doesn't waste money on unnecessary things.

2. **Start small, but be consistent:** Begin with small actions that align with your new identity. These small wins reinforce your new self-image. This is how habits are formed. Small, consistent actions are more sustainable and less overwhelming than dramatic changes. For instance, if you're shifting to a "health conscious" identity, you might start with a 10-minute workout daily. The key is consistency – doing it daily reinforces the new identity more than an occasional intense workout. I have worked out since I was 15, and when I worked out every day versus three or four days per week, I was always more consistent and also felt a lot better. You don't have to do an intense workout every day, but do something active every day to create the habit.

   These small actions serve as "identity evidence." Each time you complete the action, it's proof to yourself that you are becoming this new person. Over time, these small actions can snowball into larger changes as your new identity becomes a part of you. To become wealthier, you have to start small, too. Start by paying yourself at least 5% of your income first and investing that in a taxable investment account in low-cost ETFs (exchange-traded funds) or mutual funds, or increasing your 401k contributions past the employer match level. If you contribute 5%, increase your contributions to 8% and see how that impacts your net pay. When you get a raise, bump up your contributions instead of increasing spending on your lifestyle.

3. **Use identity-based affirmations:** Instead of saying, "I want to save money," say, "I am a person who makes wise financial decisions." What you say to yourself shapes who you become. If you are a person who makes wise financial decisions, you will start to think about decisions around your finances differently. If you are at the store about to buy a shiny new object you don't need, you will make a wiser choice if you see yourself as someone who makes wise financial decisions.

4. **Surround yourself with role models:** Spend time with people who embody the identity you're trying to have. Their influence will shape your beliefs and behaviors. They say you become the average of the five people you hang around the most. Hang around people who are health conscious. Hang around people who are wealthier than you or are good with their money. Ask them questions. Get their advice.

5. **Change your environment:** Your surroundings shape your behavior more than willpower ever will. If you're trying to save money, but your Instagram feed is full of luxury lifestyle influencers, you're going to have a hard time not wanting shiny new things or products you don't need. If you're trying to eat healthier, but your pantry is stocked with processed snacks, you're going to have a tough time making the right choices every day. Change your environment to set yourself up to be more successful with your health, life, and financial goals.

6. **Reframe setbacks:** When you slip, don't see it as proof that change is too hard. Instead, view it as an opportunity to realign with your new identity. You are going to have setbacks. That is just the reality with any new changes you make to your life. Learn from them and get back on your path to becoming this new version of yourself. Don't beat yourself up when you miss a workout or make a bad financial decision. You are human. Just get back on track to working on this new version of yourself.

7. **Celebrate progress:** Acknowledge the ways you're already becoming your new identity, no matter how small. Be proud of yourself for putting away 10% of your income before you pay the bills. Go out for a nice dinner if you meet your fitness goals for the week. Have special rewards if you follow your plan for 30, 60, or 90 days.

True transformation is not just about changing your actions; it's about changing your beliefs about yourself. As your identity changes, achieving your health or financial goals becomes less about forcing yourself to follow rules and more about expressing who you have become.

By focusing on identity change, you create a powerful internal drive that guides you toward your goals, even when motivation fades or obstacles come up. This leads to more sustainable progress in your health and financial journey.

When we consistently act in ways that align with a new identity, our self-perception shifts to match those actions. This creates what experts call a positive feedback loop where our new identity reinforces the behaviors, and the behaviors confirm your new standards. All right, this might sound too scientific, but as we repeatedly have these new thoughts and behaviors, we create and strengthen neural pathways that support our new identity. Over time, these new ways of thinking and acting become our new default. It is the science of the mind. These new pathways in our mind help us to basically build a new brain. A brain that is on your side, and you're going to need it to be on your side and not talk you out of making changes. Your brain wants you to stay in your comfort zone and keep you safe.

Identity Change with Health Example

Consider someone aiming to adopt a healthy diet. Instead of just saying, "I'm trying to eat better," they might shift their identity to "I am a health-conscious person." This identity change could result in:

- Researching and finding healthy recipes.
- Joining communities of other health-conscious individuals.
- Viewing healthy eating as the norm.
- Feeling good about choices that align with this identity.
- Signing up for a healthy meal service.
- Cleaning out the pantry and getting rid of junk food.

Identity Change with Financial Goals Example

For someone aiming to become financially independent, the identity shift might be from "I'm bad with money" to "I'm a savvy investor." This could lead to:

- Regularly educating themselves about personal finance and investing.
- Paying themselves first a percentage of their income to savings and investments.
- Seeking out mentors or role models who have achieved financial independence or financial freedom.
- Viewing being frugal as a path to financial freedom rather than being tight with money.

How Identity Change Differs from Traditional Goal Setting

Traditional goal setting often focuses on outcomes (e.g., "lose 30 pounds," "save $20,000"). While these are important, they don't address the underlying beliefs and self-image that drive long-term behavior.

Identity-based change shifts the focus from having something to being someone. Instead of "I want to have a fit body," it becomes "I am an active, healthy person." This shift is more sustainable because:

- It's internally motivated rather than external.
- It's more resilient to slip ups or setbacks because it is a mindset.
- It often leads to positive changes in other areas of life.

By focusing on identity you're not just working toward a goal, but evolving into a person for whom achieving and maintaining that goal is just an expression of who they are.

Changes in identity can lead to changes in behavior and mindset in different areas of life too. I know for me, becoming a health-conscious person has helped me with confidence, energy, and goal setting in other areas of my life. When I work out, everything else falls into place easier. I eat healthier. I have more energy. I am more disciplined in other areas of my life.

Transforming your life, your health, or your wealth requires first a shift in your self-image and how you view yourself. Once you start taking action as this new person, you will have a better chance to reach all your long-term goals related to your health, your wealth, and your life.

This chapter, as well as the information in Chapter 2, are essential to understand and will help you create your M.A.D.E. Life Action Plan in Chapter 9 to help you reach your most important life, health, and financial goals without your past identity and beliefs in your way.

MOMENTOUS DECLARATION #1

I will make health my priority because I want to live a long, active life filled with experiences and enjoy the wealth I create.

MOMENTOUS DECLARATION #2

My past has nothing to do with the future I can create for myself and my family.

CHAPTER TWO

IDENTIFYING YOUR MONEY AND HEALTH BLOCKS

I've always loved the quote from Napoleon Hill's book *Think and Grow Rich*. He said, "There is a difference between wishing for a thing and being ready to receive it. No one is ready for a thing until he believes he can acquire it. The state of mind must be belief, not mere hope or wish. Open-mindedness is essential for belief." He also said, "There are no limitations to the mind except those that we acknowledge."

Something may be getting in your way with building and keeping your wealth or improving your health. It concerns what you believe, think, and expect regarding money and health.

One of the major blocks to financial freedom or better health is our mindset about those things. When we release those blocks and become self-aware about our own personal relationship with money and our health, we can begin to rewrite our own personal story. Identifying some of these money or health blocks is a crucial step toward financial security and a healthier life.

Blocks may arise from limiting beliefs, a fear of failure, or past financial hardships, and they can really hinder your ability to thrive financially or reach your fitness or health goals. Money blocks are a real obstacle, and so are blocks around your ability to lose weight for good or improve your health long-term. Some of us have faced them in the past; some of us are facing them right now, and we don't even realize it.

It can be difficult to recognize that a money block is the root cause of some of your financial issues. It can also be difficult to understand these issues may be causing you to not make progress on your health.

What I hope you'll get from this chapter is maybe an aha! moment after reading and realizing that your money block has prevented you from reaching financial success. Your block around health is also preventing you from sticking with a healthy lifestyle routine.

MONEY BLOCKS

Most people believe that merely changing their financial habits is enough to stop them from being broke, but that isn't always the case.

So, what is a money block?

A money block is a series of thoughts or beliefs around money. It's a mindset or a feeling that gets in the way of you accomplishing financial success. It could be preventing you from getting out of debt. It could be preventing you from saving money. It could be preventing you from getting a better job that has a higher income or leading you to live a lifestyle above your means. There are things like financial therapy, mindset coaching, and establishing some realistic financial goals that can really empower you to conquer some of these obstacles in your way.

By addressing these money blocks and shifting your mindset regarding money, you can change your financial life for the better. This is not something that we all think about very often. Our thoughts influence everything in our life, our personal relationships, our family life, and our success at work, but they're also very important when it comes to money.

Your thoughts shape your beliefs, your attitudes, and ultimately your actions. When you constantly think negative thoughts, you might find that you may have more negative experiences as your mind has become kind of attuned to focusing on the negative. We all know those people who are always negative, and they always seem to have something bad going on in their lives. Yes, some circumstances are tough, and bad things happen to good people, but a lot of times our thoughts are really creating some of those bad experiences in our lives, including when it comes to money.

On the other end of the spectrum, we know those people who are always positive. They always seem to have great things going on in their life, and they never seem to complain about where they are financially, or their job, or their personal relationships.

So here are three steps to overcome some of your money blocks.

Step 1: Identify that you have some type of money block.

Take time to reflect on the money beliefs you hold. Some of those beliefs are not really yours. You didn't create those. Those were created early in your childhood, either from a parent, a teacher, or someone of influence. Those attitudes and beliefs are often ingrained from past experiences. They shape your attitude toward money, and they influence a lot of the financial decisions that you're making today.

I want you to take some time to reflect on your beliefs surrounding money and ask yourself, are they serving you well? Do they align with your financial goals? By looking at some of these money beliefs, you can make really intentional changes to cultivate a more positive and prosperous relationship with money.

So, let's just talk about some of the common money blocks that you might have thought yourself or heard someone else say. I've often heard people say, "I just can't seem to make enough," "I just make enough to pay the bills," "I can't afford that," "There's no way I can save money," or "I just can't seem to get out of debt." And then you might have heard other people say things like, "Money doesn't grow on trees." "Greed is bad." "Money is the root of all evil." Or you just might say something as simple as, "I never have any money." I remember reading in some self-development books where someone said that if your goal is just to make enough to pay the bills, that is exactly what you'll do. Make just enough to pay the bills.

These are just some of the money blocks that we've maybe had. To combat some of these past money blocks or negative thoughts, it's important to be aware of them and then try to change them. And over time, this process will become automatic. Instead of focusing on what you can't do, you will shift your mindset to abundance and focus on what you can do.

Step 2:   Challenge your negative beliefs.

Once you've identified some of those negative money beliefs or money blocks, I want you to challenge them. Are they based on facts, or are they based on irrational fears or incomplete truths? Irrational fears are things we think could happen. It's not that they may not be valid, but they tend to create an emotional response that leads to self-defeating behaviors that make financial problems more likely rather than less.

Incomplete truths often are based upon our personal experiences or something we heard from someone of influence in our life. They may have some factual basis, but leave out important details and draw from our past perspectives around money. They are usually based on assumptions we have regarding money. It's like seeing only a single puzzle piece, rather than the whole picture.

Some irrational fears might be:

1. I could lose everything.
2. If I look at my checking account, there will be bad news.
3. If I become wealthy, I'll change or become a bad person.

4. People may judge me for being frugal.
5. Making more money will solve all of my problems.
6. I don't understand money and never will.

Some incomplete truths might be:

1. Money can't buy happiness.
2. Rich people are greedy.
3. If you work hard, you will be rich.
4. More money means less stress.
5. Having debt is always bad.
6. Living frugally means you're good with money.

You need to identify these past money beliefs and challenge them. Make a more empowering belief or mindset. Instead of saying, "I can't afford that," ask, "How can I afford that?" I can afford that and will figure out how to make it happen.

Instead of saying, "I just can't seem to get ahead," say something like, "I have the education skills and tools to get a better job, do a side hustle, save money, and succeed financially."

Instead of saying, "I just make enough to pay the bills," reframe that and say, "I can create opportunities and I'll find ways to make more money on top of my bills to save for the future."

Instead of saying, "I lost so much money investing in stocks before," reframe that and say, "I've learned from my mistakes and I have more tools, more education, and more skills to become a better investor."

Instead of saying that saving and money are the root of all evil, flip that and look at all the good things that you could do with money in your life, whether that's donating to charity, saving for the future, or helping your kids or grandkids with college.

Sometimes our relationship with money is just all about how we talk about it. My good friend Shawn Carlin has an X page called MindMaven, where he talks about mindset. He posted something one day that really hit me. He said, "Why don't you and money get along? Your wealth is suffering because of it. Your money blocks are making you pissed at anyone that has money and, at the same time, keeping you from attaining it." The key to money abundance is to heal your relationship with money.

When I saw that post from Shawn, it brought me back to my 20s when I was struggling to build a financial practice from scratch, and I was making a small commission check. I'd see other friends who had gotten jobs out of college doing much better than me. I wasn't pissed at my friends, but I looked around and saw other people who appeared to be more successful. I was comparing my situation to their situations. It really got to me, probably preventing me from achieving some success until I started to realize that more was possible and if I just kept working hard, changed my mindset, stopped comparing myself to others, I could achieve my long-term goals. When I shifted my thinking about what was possible for me, everything changed. I created a three-year vision and took action each day and stopped comparing myself to others on where I was financially. I started focusing on what I could do and where I would be three years from then or five years from then if I just put my blinders on and did the work each and every day.

Step 3:   Create financial goals.

Some of these money blocks can be related to not having specific goals. They could be related to just not forgiving yourself for maybe some past money mistakes. But it also can be from just avoiding finances in general. Sometimes, people don't want to deal with money, or they say something like, "Oh, I'm just not good with money." They avoid their finances, and they never seem to find a way to get ahead. Avoiding your finances is the worst thing that you can possibly do. You need to get in the habit of constantly checking in with your money, creating a net worth report, and following your progress. If you haven't started saving for the future, it will take time for things to compound for you to really start seeing the results.

It's a lot like working out. If you go to the gym for three months, you might not see much visible progress. Most people quit before they see the progress that the hard work can do for them. They quit right before things can really start to compound.

It's the same with money; it takes time to build your wealth. You need to check in with your money and create some goals. So, set some financial goals. Identify some of your objectives, assess your current situation, and create a budget that balances living for today with saving for the future. Establish an emergency fund account and educate yourself before you invest. Then, monitor your progress and adjust things as you go along. You will learn crucial wealth principles to apply to your life in Chapters 5–7, which will give you the tools to create new standards that can dramatically improve your financial situation over time.

HEALTH BLOCKS: OBSTACLES TO BECOMING HEALTHIER

Many people aspire to lead healthier lives but struggle to make lasting changes. These limiting beliefs or "health blocks" can be a significant barrier to achieving our health goals. Understanding and addressing these blocks is crucial to improving our health long-term.

Here are some common health blocks:

1. Limiting beliefs

Our mindset plays a crucial role in our health journey. Negative self-talk and beliefs like "I'll never be fit" or "Healthy food is boring" can sabotage our efforts before we even begin. I can tell you from experience that once you start eating healthy, you will crave healthy foods. Eating healthy is not boring unless you make it that way by eating the same thing every day. If you don't think you will ever be fit, you probably won't. If you think you can, and have a plan and strong reasons to become healthier, you will.

Here are some of the most common limiting beliefs about our health:

1. "I don't have the right genetics to be fit" – This ignores how lifestyle changes can dramatically impact health regardless of genetics. It may be harder for some, but thinking this belief will keep you stuck.

2. "I'm too old/young to start getting healthy" – Health improvements can begin at any age, and studies show exercise benefits people of all ages.

3. "Eating healthy is too expensive" – While some healthy foods can be more costly, there are many options that are affordable, especially when compared to processed foods or dining out.

4. "I need to do everything perfectly or it's not worth doing" – This all-or-nothing thinking prevents people from making sustainable incremental changes or even starting in the first place.

5. "I'll have to give up my social life to be healthy" – This ignores how health goals can be integrated into a fun social life.

6. "I've failed before, so I'll fail again" – This block mistakes the past as a predictor of the future, rather than seeing them as learning experiences. If you tried diets and they didn't work, you may have a negative view of diets and never try again.

2. Lack of time

In our busy lives, finding time for exercise or meal preparation can seem impossible. If we use lack of time as an excuse, this leads to never figuring out how we can make the time to live healthier. If you have two hours at the end of the day to binge watch Netflix, you have time to be active or work out and make healthy meals. If you don't have time to cook because you have two kids in traveling soccer like me, then meal plan on Sundays or use a healthy food service to deliver meals to you each week.

3.   Stress and emotional eating

Many use food as a coping mechanism for stress, leading to some unhealthy eating patterns. This type of block is not always easy to overcome, but you can replace what you eat when you are stressed, or instead of sitting on the couch, go for a walk or meditate.

4.   Information overload

The abundance of health advice can be paralyzing, making it difficult to know where to start. As a certified health and life coach, I have learned a lot about what works and what doesn't when it comes to eating healthy and changing your habits. I am not a nutritionist, but I have some wisdom to share with you, which I discuss in the chapter on the top 10 health decisions to live a richer life.

5.   Lack of patience

Most people don't stick to eating healthy or a fitness routine because they don't commit to it long enough to see the results. They quit too easily because the results don't show up soon enough. Health habits compounded over time act just like compound interest, they will begin to improve and strengthen you the longer you keep up a healthy lifestyle.

6.   Lack of motivation

Without a clear, compelling reason for change it's easy to lose motivation on our health journey. Most people think they need to get motivated, and they will do the things they need to do to become healthier. But motivation precedes action. If you take action, you will become more motivated. You have to have a why behind your why to stay motivated long-term, which I will discuss later in the book.

You will learn essential health principles to apply to your life in Chapter 8, which will help you improve your health mindset and give you the tools to create a healthier life.

So what I want you to do over the next week is think about what some of your money blocks may be and what some of your past limiting beliefs may be about money. Also, think about your limiting beliefs regarding your health and fitness. Write them down and reframe those limiting beliefs into positive and empowering ones.

By taking control of your finances and health, I think you can overcome some of that money or health avoidance behavior that you've had in the past or some of the money or health blocks that are in your way to create financial freedom and a healthy life. Now it's time to define what a rich life means to you.

MOMENTOUS DECLARATION #3

My beliefs are nothing more than a thought I have kept thinking and I can change my thoughts, therefore I can change my beliefs.

MOMENTOUS DECLARATION #4

Money has no emotions. It does not have energy. Humans do; therefore I can change the emotions and energy I have around money.

CHAPTER THREE

DESIGNING YOUR RICH LIFE

"The real measure of our wealth is how much we'd be worth if we lost all our money."

– John Henry Jowett

A rich life is different for everyone. It's not just about money. It is about living a richer life of meaning and experiences, and making a difference. If you want a better life, some important decisions must be made. Ask yourself: Three years from now, five years from now, or 10 years from now, do you want to think and feel the same things?

One of the most powerful exercises I learned through my health and life coach certification process was an exercise in intuitive decision-making. Intuitive decision-making is a process that involves the mind and body connection. We may have heard the expression that the body doesn't lie.

The exercise involves helping you make a decision you are faced with right now in your life. An example of two decisions might be a decision to stay at your current job or a decision to go off on your own and start your own company. The exercise involves six steps:

Step 1: Stand up and visualize a place where there are five feet in front of you, both to your left and right. The space you are currently in is a neutral space.

Step 2: In your mind's eye, take one of the decisions and place it in front of you to your right and take the other decision and mark that out to your left.

Step 3: Take a step into the right area and think about that decision. Visualize that you have made this decision, it's done, and now you are living in that option. Take a moment to feel what it feels like to have made this decision, and you are experiencing the results. Take a deep breath and let your body feel what it's like, hear what it's like, and fully experience it. Notice the emotions in your body.

Step 4: After a minute or two, step back into the neutral space. Shake it out. You repeat this process for the other decision, but you step into the spot on the left. Do steps 2–4 for the decision you placed to the left.

Step 5: After you are back in the neutral space and have relaxed a bit, what did you notice about stepping into the decisions on your right and your left? What was different about the two decisions? How did you feel and what did you learn about each of those decisions?

Step 6: Ask yourself if you are ready to make a decision now and what decision feels the best.

During this process with a client, you could tell which decision felt the best by their body language. They might have tensed up, looked stressed, or breathed differently. The body doesn't lie. Unfortunately, I don't have you in front of me to run through this exercise with you, but you can try it on your own using the six steps.

Think about the momentous decisions you need to make right now. What would it feel like three, five, 10 years from now if you made some decisions today to better your life, your wealth, and your health, so that three, five or 10 years from now, you are not thinking or feeling the same things? Now what would it feel like if you didn't?

I did workshops in 2015 and 2016 to help the advisors of the brokerage firm I was at live a better, more balanced life and meet their business goals, as well as their life goals. In 2016, I set up a three-hour workshop for our region. My wife Amie was struggling with some stomach pain and back pain at the time, and she was slotted to see the doctor on the same day I was doing the workshop. The workshop happened to be about developing a compelling vision for your life, which I had created myself, and I was teaching others how to create this better, more compelling vision for their life. Little did I know that the news that we would find out two weeks later would upend our whole life.

In 2016, Amie was diagnosed with pancreatic cancer, and 10 months later, she was gone. So, this compelling vision that I had for my life was completely disrupted. And here I am seven years later, still trying to figure out life. But I feel like when I look back at the experience of losing my wife and the mother of my children, I recognize that all the self-development work I did before that had really helped me get through one of the hardest things I have ever had to go through. I grieved, I reflected, I listened to my heart, and when my mind was somewhat clear, I started envisioning how I could live a more fulfilling life in honor of her, for my kids and for myself. I knew one day I would have to create a new vision for my life.

Today, I have a philosophy on life, health, and wealth called the M.A.D.E. Life Philosophy. It's all about designing a way to live a richer life. It's an acronym for meaning, accomplishment, difference, and experiences. The M.A.D.E. Life Philosophy is focused on the fact that I believe experiences are more important than things. I believe that strong relationships should be centered around the three As. The three As are attention, affection, and appreciation. I believe your health is paramount in being able to enjoy your wealth. I believe that having a financial plan can contribute to your overall well-being. I believe that living with intention leads to more fulfillment and joy. I believe that giving back is a priceless life experience. And I believe that comfort is the enemy of achievement. I've been very comfortable many times in my life, and I've gone sideways, and I don't like that feeling of not making progress. However, the most important philosophy to living a richer life is understanding the why behind your why. That will keep you inspired long-term to reach your personal goals, your life goals, your relationship goals, and your wealth and money goals. Ten, 20, or 30 years from now, you're going to look back at your life and reflect and ask yourself, what did I make of my life?

That's where this M.A.D.E. Life Framework comes into play, looking at what gave your life meaning, what things you accomplished, what difference you made, and what experiences you had along the way.

To design a richer life requires you, first of all, to be grateful for what you've done so far. A really helpful exercise I used to have people do in workshops is to look at the 10-year history of good things.

What you do is you take out a sheet of paper, or you make a note on your phone, list the year ten years previous, write your age, and just list some of the good things that you did or accomplished in that year and also some of the experiences you had. Having the year and your age will jog your memory to reflect on all the good things that you've done and accomplished in your life so far. Keep going with this list for each year until the current year. When you look at this 10-year history you will feel one of two things. You will feel good about the life you have lived the past 10 years or you will feel like you could have done more, become more, or things could have been a little better. It is natural to have some feeling of discontent, because you maybe wanted more for your life. Give yourself some grace and know that the past is the past. If your life was filled with great memories, friendships, and a family who loves you, your life has been rich. If you don't feel the best when you look back at the last 10 years, it may be time to change some things. It is time to design a richer life going forward.

To design a richer life going forward, you make the 10-year history of good things to come. Write down the year, your age right now, and project that out 10 years. Write down some things you want to do, whether to create more meaning, or things you want to accomplish, or maybe some charities you want to get involved with to make a difference, or some of the experiences you want to have. List some of the things that you want to do to be able to live that richer life that you know you're capable of and that you want to live. In the 7 Steps chapter, I give you a framework to develop a 10-year vision of the richer life you want to live that will create a pull in you from the future. It will take this 10-year history of good things to come and turn it into a story that will excite you and help you take action on all the things that are important to you.

You want to have a vision of your life one year from now, three years from now, five years from now, and 10 years from now, but sometimes it's overwhelming to look at this big vision of your life. That is why 90-Day plans work so well. You have a long-term vision with short-term action plans. I have a 90-Day Plan available for you to download to help you design your richer life. It's called the M.A.D.E. 90-Day Life Action Plan, and I will dive into it in more detail later in this book in the 7 Steps Chapter.

Some of us think our richer life is far in the distance, once the kids are gone, we have more money, or we retire. Why wait until retirement to live a better life? One of my good friends has been living a richer life his whole career. He has traveled the world to over 40 destinations and always extended his trips. He had a great career as a financial advisor and took great care of his clients, but he got the travel bug early and wanted to create memorable experiences while he was young and not wait until retirement. He was the guy who said he would never retire, but he finally pulled the plug and now his idea of a rich life is attending to his community garden with his wife, traveling to see their kids and grandkids in different states, and creating more meaningful relationships with good friends.

Most of us don't have the ability to travel every month or even twice a year for that matter, but we can make an effort to go on small weekend adventures, spend time with family more often for backyard barbecues, or create experiences for our kids that they will remember for a lifetime. We can create more meaning in our lives, we can accomplish our most important goals, we can make a difference with the simplest things or grand gestures, and we can focus on experiencing more as each year passes. My wish for all my clients and friends is for them to live their version of a richer life now and well into the future. That requires some life decisions, health decisions, and wealth decisions. The next three chapters will go into these in detail. It also requires knowing what you want, why you want it, and creating a vision for your life that pulls you from the future.

If you're having a tough time thinking about what you want your life to be like going forward, here are some questions to ask to help spark some things in you:

Core Identity and Values

- When do you feel most alive and energized?
- What would you regret not doing, being, or creating if this was your last year?
- What principles will you not compromise on going forward?

Purpose and Impact

- How could your work or actions positively impact others' lives?
- What legacy do you want to leave?
- What would you do if money wasn't an issue?

Growth and Learning

- What skills or knowledge would dramatically improve your life?
- What things would stretch you out of your comfort zone?
- How can you turn your failures into learning opportunities?

Relationship and Community

- Who are the people who elevate and energize you?
- How can you contribute more to your most important relationships?
- How can you create more meaningful connections?

Experience and Adventure

- Which fears would you like to overcome?
- What brings you genuine joy?
- How can you inject more fun and curiosity into your life?

Well-being and Energy Management

- What activities restore your energy?
- How can you design your environment to support your goals?
- What boundaries do you need to protect your well-being?

Achievement

- What would you like to excel at?
- What achievements would give you a sense of pride?
- What systems or disciplines would support your goals?

Creating a better life comes down to knowing what you want, which I discuss more in detail in the first step of Designing a Richer Life in the 7 Steps chapter. I will give you a framework for describing your ideal life and helping you create new standards and a vision for your future.

MOMENTOUS DECLARATION #5

I am focused on designing a richer life rather than just making a living.

CHAPTER FOUR

LIFE DECISIONS FOR A RICHER LIFE

Before you can take the steps to experience a richer life, you need to make some important decisions about your life, your wealth, and your health. So, let's start with your life. I am sure there are hundreds of decisions you could make, and maybe you have some that are important to you that are not on this list, but these are just some of those I have found through my self-development journey that have had the greatest impact on my life.

LIFE DECISION #1: EXPERIENCE MORE THINGS

"Experiences Are More Important Than Things"

In a world where stuff to buy is constantly in our faces, it's hard to avoid wanting new shiny objects or the latest thing. However, we all know they provide temporary pleasure; they are fleeting and can quickly lose their luster. I have an Instant Pot in my pantry I still haven't used. I have gadgets I have bought from Instagram ads that are collecting dust. I have a fat-tire electric bike that I haven't had to charge in a year because it sits in my garage most of the time. It does come in handy though, when I have to look for my kids in the neighborhood.

Experiences create lasting memories and bring you joy. Whether it's traveling to new places, trying new things, or spending time with loved ones, investing in experiences can lead to a more fulfilling and meaningful life. So, instead of accumulating more things, prioritize experiences and make memories.

I remember reading the following on the back of keycard at the Viceroy resort in Anguilla: "THIS IS WHY. Because you live in some places and in others you're alive." Maybe that is why I fell in love with Anguilla so long ago. There is something about being in the Caribbean that changes me. That makes me come alive. I feel at peace. I feel more creative. I feel more energized. But experiencing more things is not just about traveling to exotic places, it's about the little things. It's about creating more memorable moments. I have great memories setting up my backyard for outdoor movies, cooking woodfire pizzas in my Solo Stove, going glamping, playing music in my studio with the kids, having an outdoor tent birthday party for my daughter, and all of our hikes to different state parks.

Experiences are what you will remember along with the people you share those experiences with. Don't get me wrong, I like nice things. I love to travel. But I only buy things I can afford and that bring me joy and long-term happiness. And I only travel if I can afford to.

Some of my favorite experiences required little to no money. I think we all had time during Covid, as we were trapped in our homes, to find out what was most important to us. I took that time to reflect and tried to figure out fun things to do. I have played guitar since I was 15 but never learned the ukulele, so I took some online courses on the Fender app. Now, I bring my uke on every trip to write songs about my experiences. We ordered an adventure book from the adventure challenge company for $39.99 and for four weeks randomly tried a new challenge. We made a string obstacle course, stuffed a piñata and whacked away, used my black lights and strobe lights to create a roller disco in the basement. We also recorded songs we wrote about our feelings around the pandemic and how we wanted life to be different when it was all over. Those songs are forever burned in my mind.

Make an experience list, similar to a bucket list, of the things you want to do over the coming years, and then plan them out every 90 days. Having things planned that you can look forward to brings excitement and anticipation into your life. Leave some room for spontaneity, yet live a life by design. Living life by design means you're purposefully designing the elements of your life, from family, business, and friends, toward your definition of a richer life. It doesn't mean that your life is perfect, but it does mean that you're living intentionally and with passion, knowing exactly where you want to go and what will bring you more happiness and joy.

When Things Don't Seem to Add Up, Start Subtracting

If you add up all the things in your life that are good, but you're still not happy, think about the things you can get rid of. If spending money on material things makes you happy in the short term, but makes you feel horrible two days later (buyer's remorse), take that out of your life and replace it with something that makes you feel good long-term like putting away 10% into your financial independence account or making a travel or experience savings account. Focus on building your net worth instead of going into debt by overspending. If TV is taking up too much of your time, replace an hour of TV watching with reading something positive, or a good book, or playing cards, or a board game with your family. The average person spends 12+ years of their life watching television. Get back at least three of those years by reading or listening to music or playing fun games for an hour each night.

Here are some examples of some meaningful experiences that you can have with your family:

1. "Adventure Sundays." Each family member takes turns planning a small adventure. Have one of your kids design a neighborhood treasure hunt. Learn to make pasta from scratch. Go geocaching. Go to a new hiking spot at a local state park. Take a road trip. Draw together. Take a painting class. Plan a trip together with all the things you will do while you are there.

2. Create seasonal traditions that become part of your family story. In the spring, you might start a family garden together. In the summer you could have weekly sunset picnics at different locations. In the fall, do some apple picking and making cider from scratch. In the winter, you could craft homemade gifts for each other. We may not all have the talent of Martha Stewart, but we can try new things as a family that can become traditions.

3. A "Mystery Day" tradition. Once a month, one person plans a complete surprise day for the family. The only rule is it has to be something new for everyone.

4. Start a family book club where you read the same book. If you want to take it a step further, act out your favorite scenes.

5. Create a home "restaurant" where kids help plan the menu, decorate, and serve as waiters.

6. Have a backyard camping night and do some storytelling and stargazing.

7. Start a family time capsule project, collecting meaningful items throughout the year.

8. Buy a dart board and have a family cricket tournament.

If you want to create more experiences with your family or in your relationship, consider purchasing an adventure challenge book from theadventurechallenge.com. There are a lot of fun ideas with scratch-off adventures you can do as a family. There is also one you can buy for you and your partner to spice up your relationship.

Spend your time creating experiences rather than buying or consuming and you will feel richer with life. Things provide temporary happiness. Experiences create lasting happiness and some stories to tell. In the 7 Steps chapter you will be planning out your experiences every 90 days. You will plan simple things or rituals you will do each week or month, trips you want to get scheduled, and events like live music, comedy, or other things you are passionate about.

> **Wise Life Tip**: Create a weekly ritual of doing something special and call it something like Bonfire Fridays, or Music Mondays, or Burgers for Breakfast Saturdays. Find your something special moments and do them often.

LIFE DECISION #2: BUILD STRONG RELATIONSHIPS CENTERED AROUND THE THREE As

For the relationships we have to be meaningful and long-lasting, the three As can serve as guide. The three As are Attention, Affection, and Appreciation. Paying close attention to the other person's needs, expressing genuine affection, and showing appreciation go a long way in making and keeping strong relationships. By making an effort to prioritize the three As with those we care about, we can build deeper, more meaningful connections that stand the test of time. If something is off in your marriage or relationship, you can usually point to one of the three As.

Attention

> *"Plants do not grow merely to satisfy ambitions or to fulfill good intentions. They thrive because someone expended effort on them and gave them attention."*
>
> – Liberty Hyde Bailey

When was the last time you really gave someone your full attention? Jim Rohn often said, "The greatest gift you can give someone is the gift of your attention." When you give someone your full attention, it creates a bond that becomes very hard to break when people feel understood. When people feel listened to. We have all heard the expression, "People don't care about how much you know until they know how much you care." There are a lot of expressions to live by, but this one will always stand the test of time. Show people you care by giving them your attention and truly listening and caring, and good things will happen in your personal and professional life.

All it takes is minutes out of your day to give focused, quality attention. For example, when it comes to your relationship with your spouse, take 10 minutes in the morning to spend time talking about what they are going to do that day or what they are most excited about. Take 10 minutes out of your afternoon to connect about anything exciting that has happened or to just listen to them; take 10 minutes when you get home to give your spouse your full attention. Listen to them. Ask them how their day went. What were their thorns, and what were the roses of their day? These 30 minutes each day, as simple as it sounds and easy to do but also easy not to do, can make all the difference in the quality of your relationship. Over one year, you would have spent 10,000 minutes giving your attention to someone you care deeply about. That is less than 3% of your time in a typical day. That's just 3% of your time over the course of a year. It's 3% of your time that will keep you connected each day so that no thoughts or feelings get put off or bottled up. It doesn't require a ton of effort, but it can make a ton of difference. Something easy to do but also easy not to do. Give those you care about the gift of your attention. There is no downside, only upside. You will be glad you did.

Affection

> *"Affection is responsible for nine-tenths of whatever solid and durable happiness there is in our lives."*
>
> – C. S. Lewis

The book *Love Languages* focuses quite a bit on the importance of affection, well, at least if that is what your partner desires. Who doesn't want a little affection? If your partner has this as one of their love languages, do your thing, whatever that may be. To me, affection is being intentional about it. A small touch, rubbing your partner's shoulders or neck after a tough day, giving a long, hard hug, or kissing your partner out of the blue.

Showing your kids affection and love is also vital for their well-being and happiness. If you didn't get that from your parents, you know how that feels and how it affected you. Your kids need to know you love them with more than just words. Hug your kids and teach them how to hug. A hug is not some side hug thing that feels like you are doing it just because. It is a strong hug that lets the person know you love them.

Affection can also be really important in your friendships. A strong hug or telling those you care about you love them goes a long way. Showing compassion for their struggles can also be a form of affection. Your friends need to know you are there for them and know how important they are to you.

Appreciation

> *"Appreciation is a wonderful thing. It makes what is excellent in others belong to us as well."*
>
> – Voltaire

I met a businessman when I was a wholesaler for Hartford Mutual Funds. He had a very simple philosophy on how he treated people. Whenever he met someone, he visualized a Post-it Note above their forehead that said, "Make me feel special." I remember how he made me feel when I first met him, and I bet everyone else did too. He passed away a number of years back, and I bet everyone had the same thing to say about him.

Having a habit of showing appreciation can have an enormous positive impact in our relationships with our loved ones and the people we come in contact with. It simply takes a couple of minutes to appreciate someone. In a matter of minutes, we can literally make someone's day simply by showing our appreciation. We all have a deep need to be appreciated. It just feels good.

When was the last time you showed someone true appreciation? Appreciation can also lead to more success in your personal and professional life because of the old adage that "a person who feels appreciated will always do more than what is expected." Don't expect people always to appreciate you, but if you focus on being appreciative of other people, everything changes instantly, and they will, in turn, appreciate you.

People will never know how much you appreciate them until it's too late, so practice appreciation each day so you never have to worry about leaving someone not feeling appreciated. If you don't show appreciation to those who deserve it, they will learn to stop doing the things that are important to you that you appreciate. A moment of appreciation makes all the difference for you and all those around you.

In Hal Urban's book *Life's Greatest Lessons*, he asks the question, "If you were asked to make a list of the people you appreciate the most, wouldn't it be an easy task to write down their names? And if you were asked why you appreciate them, wouldn't it be just as easy to write the reasons after each name?" Then, he goes on to ask a more difficult question. "Could you write after each name on your list the last time you told that person you appreciate him or her?" If you take the step each day to show true appreciation, you're going to make two people feel very good: the person you're thanking and yourself.

Why do we usually only say good things about people when they're not around anymore? When someone passes away, everyone typically has something good to say. I wonder sometimes, like Hal Urban, how many of those compliments were heard by the person while they were still alive. Did we take the time to express our appreciation?

In the 7 Steps chapter you may choose to improve your most important relationships by bringing the three As into your life. Every 90 days you will focus on One Momentous Thing you can do each day, or week, to make your relationships richer.

Wise Life Tip: Show appreciation each day, and you will get it in return.

LIFE DECISION #3: PRACTICE GRATITUDE

"We seldom think of what we have but always of what we lack."
– Arthur Schopenhauer

When was the last time you felt grateful? For those you are close to? For the abundance in your life? For your talents? For your gifts? For your life? If you have food in the refrigerator, a roof over your head, and clothes on your back, you're richer than 75% of the world. We should always try to look for moments to be thankful for all the good in our lives. Grateful thoughts strengthen you. Ungrateful thoughts weaken you. Being grateful will also bring you more fulfillment and joy.

A few questions that can help you to start finding more gratitude after each day:

What is one small thing I can appreciate about what I have done today?

What is one small thing I can appreciate about what I have learned today?

What am I truly grateful for right now in my life?

How did I make a difference in someone's life today?

What accomplishment made me feel like I made progress on my vision for my life, health, or financial situation?

What did I do that made me feel like I went the extra mile for something or someone?

There Are No Ordinary Moments

I love the story of Socrates and his student. Socrates told one of his students to go sit by a rock in silence and think. He said, "When you think of something important or significant, come back and tell me." So the student sat at the rock in silence. Every time he thought he had something significant, he would stop and ask himself, "Is this important?" He finally got the courage to go tell Socrates what he thought was significant. Each time Socrates said, "No that's not important, go to back to the rock until you have thought of something significant." After three times coming back to Socrates getting the same response, he finally came back and said something that Socrates said, "Yes you have found something that is significant." What the student said was that there are "no ordinary moments." Every moment of our life is something to be grateful for. Having a spouse who was diagnosed with one of the deadliest forms of cancer with a prognosis of a year to live taught me more about life than anything else I have been faced with. There truly is so much to be grateful for that was often overlooked before. The air we breathe. The roof over our heads. Our family bonds. The health of our children. Our amazing friends. Our ability to travel to wonderful places. The clean water we drink. The country we live in. Every moment is a second chance. There are no ordinary moments.

A Gratitude Experiment That Will Change Your Life

When it comes down to it, being thankful or grateful is a habit—one of the best ones you can ever have. Being grateful will change how you look at your problems and circumstances. As they say, when you change how you look at things, the things you look at change.

So here is an experiment to do over the next 48 hours that can change your life: I discovered this in the book *Life's Greatest Lessons* by Hal Urban.

STEP 1 – THE FIRST 24 HOURS: The first exercise is simple to explain but not to do. Try to go through the next 24 hours without complaining. Do not stop the experiment if you blow it and complain within the first hour. If you can't go 24 hours without complaining, try at least to see how few complaints you can make in one day. Carry a piece of paper with you or make a note in your phone and write down each time you complain and each time you catch yourself about to complain.

This exercise will help you notice that most of the things you complain about are pretty trivial, unimportant, and unnecessary. We have all been around someone who complains a lot, and those complaints usually fall on deaf ears anyway. Complaining does nothing for you except attract more things to complain about into your life.

STEP 2 – THE SECOND 24 HOURS: Write on paper or in a note on your phone about the top things you are thankful for. Then, write down the words THINGS, PEOPLE, and OTHER. In each category, write down the things you are thankful for. When it comes to the OTHER category, examples might include freedom, opportunity, friendship, love, intelligence, abilities, health, talents, peace, faith, God, security, learning, experiences, beauty, and kindness.

Over the next 24 hours, read your list three times: after lunch, before going to sleep, and the next morning before work.

After one day, notice how different you feel compared with how you felt the day before after trying not to complain. You will notice and feel significantly different, not only from the day before but from any previous day. When we focus on what's right instead of what's wrong, life improves dramatically.

STEP 3 – NOW DO IT FOR SEVEN DAYS: Try reading your list three or four times per day for seven days straight. Practice being grateful daily, and it will make all the difference in your life.

Being grateful for what we have is one of the healthiest ways of looking at life. It takes a few minutes a day, but it can make all the difference in your life.

In the 7 Steps chapter you may choose to work on appreciating your life more and practice gratitude. Over 90 days as part of your M.A.D.E. Life Action Plan, you will focus on ONE MOMENTOUS THING you can do to bring more gratitude into your life.

> **Wise Life Tip**: Put an alarm in your phone for 10 minutes before you go to bed and label it "What I'm Thankful For." Take five minutes before you go to bed and say the things you are thankful for.

LIFE DECISION #4: BE POSITIVE, THINK POSITIVE

We have thousands of thoughts every single day. I have heard many numbers in different self-help books on how many we have every day and it is somewhere around 35,000. Obviously a lot of them are unconscious or automatic, but that is a lot of thoughts for which to guard the door of your mind. I have read also in self-help books or heard during seminars that most of those 35,000 thoughts are negative, so it is even more important for us to try to be positive or think positive. When we experience negative thoughts or emotions, they become stronger the more we let them build up inside. If we let them, they start to have a hold on us. When we have positive thoughts, they lead us to positive emotions, and we see the world through a better lens. That means we have a hard job every day. Our job is to recognize negative thoughts when they happen and try to redirect them to more empowering or positive thoughts.

I usually feel like I have control over my mindset and can get out of any funk I may be in. But in the summer of 2024, I found myself letting thoughts ruminate about lack and not feeling I was living the life I wanted. It felt a lot like depression. Nothing was feeling the same and my attitude was in the gutter. I was going through something, rather than growing through it. Nothing was wrong in my life, but for some reason I was thinking there was, and it led to feeling blah about everything. I believe what you focus on expands. When I started focusing on what was great in my life rather than what was wrong, everything started to change. I was slowly getting back to my old self. I know I have to work hard at being positive. I always have had to. I am not a naturally positive person. When I am not intentional about bringing positivity into my life with reading or listening to positive books or podcasts, or journaling about what I am grateful for, I start to revert more to the negative thoughts and habits. We all have a choice to be positive. To find the things that are great about our life. They are there. We just have to highlight them and be grateful.

Being positive is simply about adjusting your attitude. We have all heard the expression that attitude is everything. Having a positive attitude is one of the most important choices we'll ever make because it affects everything we do in life. Harvard and several other universities did a variety of different studies on attitude. The major findings were that attitude is far more important than intelligence, education, special talent, or luck. The researchers concluded that up to 85% of our success in life is due to attitude, while the other 15% is due to ability. William James, one of the most practical and respected American psychologists, said, "The greatest discovery of my generation is that human beings can alter their lives by altering their attitudes."

Earl Nightingale described attitudes as reflections of people. "What goes on inside each of us will show on the outside. It will be reflected in what we say and do." It comes down to this. A good attitude gets good results; a bad attitude gets bad results.

As Hal Urban said in his book *Life's Greatest Lessons*, "We can't adjust situations to fit our lives perfectly, but we can adjust our attitudes to fit all situations. We can do this because having a positive attitude is a learned trait. We learn either bad attitudes through repetition or our environment and we do the same with good attitudes." Hang around someone with a bad attitude for a long time, and you will soon have one of your own.

In Victor Frankl's book *Man's Search for Meaning*, he said, "we can direct our thoughts to work for us or to work against us. They can be our best friends or our worst enemies." They can attract the right people to us, or they can drive people away from us. Having the right attitude each day attracts people to you. Everyone would rather be around a person with a positive attitude rather than a negative one.

In Shad Helmstetter's book *The Gift*, he says, "When you look for it, you can see your own attitude. You can see it the first thing in the morning when you wake up. You can see it in the mirror when you're getting ready for the day. You can see it at breakfast. You can see it at work, when you're with other people, or when you're by yourself. And you can especially see it when you're confronted with the challenges or the problems of the day. If you were to study your attitude carefully, you would find that more than anything else, it is your attitude – at any given moment – that is choosing how well your day is working. And if you add all of those moments together (all of your days and weeks and months of attitude moments), you would find that more than anything around you, it is your attitude that has been choosing how well your life has been working."

Where we are today is the result of the attitudes we choose daily. Live by the old saying, "If you don't like something, change it. If you can't change it, change your attitude."

In the 7 Steps chapter you may choose to work on things to bring more positivity into your life by focusing on your emotional health or personal growth. Over 90 days as part of your M.A.D.E. Life Action Plan, you will focus on One Momentous Thing you can do to bring more positivity into your life or something to aid in your emotional health.

> **Wise Life Tip**: Before you go to bed, think about what you are excited about tomorrow. Say to yourself, I am going to wake up with a good attitude and bring my best self to my day.

LIFE DECISION #5: LIVE WITH INTENTION

"When you live each day with intentionality, there's almost no limit to what you can do. You can transform yourself, your family, your community, and your nation."

– John Maxwell

Living with intention means making a conscious effort to align your actions, thoughts, and beliefs with your values and goals. It involves being aware of your choices and taking steps toward creating your desired life. When you live with intention, you are more likely to experience a sense of purpose, fulfillment, and joy in your daily life. This is because you are working toward creating a life rather than simply going through the motions. By living intentionally, you will have greater clarity, focus, and direction, leading to a deeper sense of satisfaction and happiness.

After my wife, Amie, died in 2017, everything was different. Everything felt different. Even sunny days didn't seem that sunny. Everything felt gray. Music didn't sound the same. Food didn't taste the same. I was in a fog. I was deep in grief, and I couldn't find joy until I found a journaling exercise called Three Moments of Joy. Every day, I journaled in the morning about my Three Moments of Joy from the day before. What it started to do for me was forcing me to be intentional about looking for joy each day so that I had something to write down in my journal the next day. As each day went on, I got better at finding joy or creating it. It was all those simple moments that I was missing before because I wasn't looking for them or appreciating the moments when they happened.

You also have to be intentional about your trade-offs. Eric Hoffer said, "people will cling to an unsatisfactory way of life rather than change in order to get something better for fear of getting something worse." Why would we be okay with unsatisfactory? That is not what we really want. We want a better life, but we are just more afraid of getting something worse. I can tell you right now that being intentional about being better or creating joy will never get you something worse. The trade-offs we need to make will be small in the beginning, but the payoffs will be large in the end.

What are you willing to give up? As they say, the price of anything is exchanging part of your life for it. Some trade-offs are just not worth the price. Family time, for instance, should never be a trade-off for personal gain. Sometimes, we will have to make a choice, but if family is truly a priority, it should never be jeopardized by a trade-off.

It has been said, "We don't always get what we want; we get what we choose." Do we change now, or do we change when we have to? I would rather choose to change now, in advance of having to. Changing "before" you have to is very hard but will lead to the largest strides toward living a richer life. Changing "when" you have to might cause you to change for the better, but because it is reactive, it puts you in a position of feeling forced to change, and no one likes to be forced to change. Changing "after" you have to is after the fact. Too late. The opportunity is missed.

Know your trade-offs. Make changes now before you are forced to. Be intentional with everything, whether it is finding or looking for joy, how you talk to yourself and others, your health and wealth habits, and you will start to have a richer life.

In the 7 Steps chapter you may choose to work on being more intentional about bringing joy into your life by starting a new or old hobby. Over 90 days as part of your M.A.D.E. Life Action Plan, you will focus on One Momentous Thing you can do to bring more joy into your life.

Wise Life Tip: Journal each morning your Three Moments of Joy from the day before. This will get your mind focused on finding or creating more joy each day.

LIFE DECISION #6: GIVING BACK

"Service to others is the rent you pay for your room here on earth."

– Mohammed Ali

One of the most fulfilling experiences in life is giving back to others. Whether volunteering at a local charity, donating to a cause you believe in, or simply being there for someone in need, giving can bring a sense of purpose and joy. The feeling of making a positive impact on someone's life, even in a small way, can create a ripple effect of kindness and generosity that spreads far beyond whatever you do.

Giving back doesn't have to cost money. It just costs a small amount of your time. Giving back can be as simple as just a random act of kindness. For example, one act of kindness can impact more than just one other person, especially if that person decides to pay it forward. If you are kind to one person, they may be kind to someone else and the next thing you know your one act of kindness impacted tens or even hundreds of people. Imagine you did that every day to a new person over a one-year period and thousands of people could be affected by your one act of kindness.

When my wife passed away in 2017 from pancreatic cancer, I remember going to a church service, and, as always, the sermon felt like it was directed right at me. The pastor talked about turning your pain into purpose. He said, "You have to use this before you lose this." The next week, I started the process of setting up a 501(c)3 in honor of my wife. I started the Amie Muller Foundation to help other veteran families living with a pancreatic cancer diagnosis and to raise awareness of the veterans exposed to toxic burn pits in Iraq and Afghanistan. Over the next five years, we raised over $100,000 and helped over 20 families in need to lessen the financial burden of fighting a disease that very few are able to beat. As hard as it was to relive my wife's fight through the experience of other families, it was very fulfilling knowing we were making a small difference. The foundation was also instrumental in getting the PACT Act signed into law in 2022, thanks to the driving force of Amie's best friend and Air Force Veteran, Julie Tomaska, and Minnesota Senator Amy Klobuchar. The PACT Act expands VA health care and benefits for veterans exposed to burn pits, Agent Orange, and other toxic substances. I know Amie is looking down proud of what her life and story did to create positive changes to help veterans get the benefits and help they deserve.

I also became an ambassador for the Park Nicollet Growing Through Grief program, where we raised money using a song I wrote that was inspired by my son Jace called "Ladder To The Sky." This was very fulfilling because the Growing Through Grief program was very important to my kids' grief journey and I think it should be in every school.

You can read about the "Ladder To The Sky" story at: https://www.cbsnews.com/minnesota/news/song-about-missing-a-loved-one-helps-kids-going-through-grief.

Releasing that song, which was inspired by a dream my son had about wanting to see his mom again, sparked my love for songwriting again, and I went on to release seven more songs about life, love, grief, and personal growth. I hope those songs inspired or helped someone in their own journey.

Any time there is an event for a cause, make an effort to be a part of it or contribute if you can. Get on the board of an organization you are passionate about. Volunteer at your church when they do food drives. Give the bikes your kids have outgrown to a neighbor who has younger kids. Educate people on what you do without expecting something in return. Give back every chance you can, and your life will be richer knowing you made a difference. Giving back is a priceless life experience.

In the 7 Steps chapter you will learn more about the M.A.D.E. LifePlan and may choose to focus on giving back and generosity. Over 90 days as part of your M.A.D.E. Life Action Plan, you will focus on ONE MOMENTOUS THING you can do to give back.

Wise Life Tip: Find a cause you care about and get involved by volunteering your time.

LIFE DECISION #7: DON'T GET TOO COMFORTABLE

"You might occasionally feel that some people are standing in the way and slowing your progress, but in reality, the biggest person standing in your way is you. Others can stop you temporarily, but you are the only one who can do it permanently."

– Zig Ziglar

One of the biggest obstacles in your mind is getting trapped in your comfort zone. One of my favorite quotes is "Comfort is the enemy of achievement." It is easy to become comfortable with our current situation. We are doing good, making a decent living, and things are fine. We can get comfortable in a particular job or relationship or salary level, so much so that we become just plain reluctant to make any changes, even if those changes are for the better.

If you get too comfortable with your current situation, you tend to become complacent and unmotivated. This bleeds into every area of our life, from our finances, to our relationships, to our health. It is easy to fall into a routine when you're comfortable, but this can hinder your progress and prevent you from reaching your full potential. Achieving great things often requires stepping out of your comfort zone and taking risks. If you never challenge yourself or push beyond your limits, you will never know what you are truly capable of achieving. Jim Rohn often said, "We are trapped by either the regret of the past or the routine of the present." We're so busy with the routine of the present we don't give much thought to designing a better future.

You have complete control over the direction that the rest of your life takes. What makes the difference in how things turn out in our lives? Well, it's us. Jim Rohn would say, "If the how was the answer, it would be done. It's how you do the 'hows' that's most important. If access to the best information were the answer, we'd all be wealthy, healthy, happy, and more fulfilled. And most of us are just one of those things." The secret ingredient, according to Mr. Rohn, is your philosophy. The philosophy you create on how you want your life to go and the things you are going to do each day, no matter what, to achieve your version of a richer life. Your mindset and philosophy are changing the way you think about simple everyday things. If you don't change how you think about these simple everyday things then no amount of how's will make a difference.

There is a Zig Ziglar quote I have always loved, and it rings in my head from time to time: "Success is not about what you get; it is about who you become." If you become more, you will have more. Period.

Getting Motivated and Staying Motivated

Everyone talks about being motivated, or we say things like, "I just need to get motivated." If you're waiting to become motivated to do something, you may be waiting for a long time. Sometimes, you have to act in spite of not having motivation. Have you ever noticed a week when you were taking action, and what that does to your motivation? The old saying that things in motion tend to stay in motion is also true with your daily activity. If you don't act, you lose momentum. More action leads to more results. More results lead to more belief. More belief leads to more potential you see in yourself. The more potential you see in yourself, the more action you take, which in turn leads to even greater results, and the cycle keeps building. This is what is referred to as the Success Cycle. More success brings greater success.

Fear of Failure

One of the biggest things holding most people back is fear. Fear of the unknown. Fear of failure. Fear of committing to something not working out. The purpose of setting goals in life is to stretch you and cause you to act in spite of your fears and to get you out of your comfort zone. You may have heard this expression, "To get something you've never had, you have to do something you've never done," but the fact is, stretching yourself beyond what's comfortable and familiar can sometimes feel pretty damn scary. The bigger the goal, the more fear sets in and can almost paralyze you. But what is interesting is that the sensations of fear and excitement are pretty much the same. Our heart begins to race. Our chest might feel a little tight. So fear and excitement are very similar, but one makes you anxious, and the other leaves you ready to take on the world. The trick is transforming your fear into excitement.

You can reframe what you're experiencing as excitement rather than fear and then do what has often been said: "Feel the fear and do it anyway." The choice to choose excitement instead of fear is always yours. Fear will either be something you overcome or something that overcomes you. Fear is really just a voice in your head – a very powerful voice that you can either listen to or ignore.

The Three Enemies of Achievement

There will always be things standing in your way. The enemies of achievement show up in our lives quite often. I know they do for me. The three enemies are:

1. Lack of Discipline
2. Lack of Commitment
3. Lack of Belief

1. Lack of Discipline

> *"Discipline is doing what you should do, when you should do it, whether you feel like it or not."*
>
> – Thomas Huxley

Motivating yourself, setting goals, and working hard will take you very far in life, but when you add self-discipline, you will go even further. Some people think self-discipline is something to be avoided because it has such a negative feeling when it is said. We think of it as some sort of punishment.

Discipline is about training yourself to do what you need to do to get things done. It is about molding yourself into a better version of yourself so you can reach your goals. It is about becoming stronger and more able to take what life throws at you. When you practice discipline, you begin to realize that you are in control. You control the direction of your life. You determine what you can accomplish. You decide what you'll make of your life.

I like Hal Urban's definition of self-discipline from his book *Life's Greatest Lessons*. He says self-discipline is "getting yourself to do something, even though you don't feel like it, because the reward for getting it done far exceeds the temporary unpleasantness of the task itself."

You cannot change your life and get out of your comfort zone unless you change something that you do every day. It has been said that there are 999 success principles, but without self-discipline, none of them will work. The word discipline has a cringe-like impact when read or said out loud. To some of us, we look at discipline as a task. I know I did early on in my weightlifting days, but today I look at discipline as simply how I show up each day. If you show up engaged and excited to take on the day, it becomes much easier to be disciplined.

Make Discipline Easy at First

If you feel like you don't have enough discipline, you have to find a way to make discipline easy at first. Start the day by drinking two glasses of water and you are already a quarter of the way to drinking the amount of water you need for the day. Start the day with a healthy meal, and you will more likely be inclined to make healthy choices for the rest of the day. Begin the day with a plan with your crucial three priorities planned out and you have nothing in your way, no way to make excuses for what to do to start your day. If you show up ready to take on the day, you will start to enjoy the process of discipline, and something awesome will happen. You will actually want to do it again tomorrow. You will want to be disciplined. And when you have the motivation to be more disciplined, that means you will achieve more and, in turn, this will make you want to do it even more. Successes build on success. Do the things that are easy to do, and the harder things will become easier. Unfortunately, the things that are easy to do are also easy not to do. It's easy to get 7–8 hours of sleep per night, well, that is if you don't have insomnia, but it is also easy to be tempted to stay up late to watch the Late Show and sleep in. It's easy to set an alarm to get up at 5 a.m., but it's also very easy to hit the snooze or turn it off altogether. You have to have reasons to do the things you need to do to have a better chance of more of the things you want out of your life. You have to create an environment that will help you be more disciplined.

Ask yourself right now, "What three disciplines would make this the best year ever if I followed them? Eat healthy? Wake up early? Plan tomorrow today? Time-block? Show appreciation and gratitude? Read 30 minutes per day?"

Now start with one and figure out all the things you can do to make it easier to do. For example: If you want to start eating healthy, here are some things you could do to make it easier to do:

1. Drink two glasses of water to start your day. Easy to do.
2. Get rid of all the junk in the pantry. Easy to do, well, except those Oreos.
3. Buy some fresh vegetables, brown rice instead of white, and yams or sweet potatoes instead of baked potatoes. It's easy to do, but it's not easy to get used to.
4. Drink one glass of water before each meal to prevent yourself from eating too much at each sitting. Easy to do and probably the most important simple thing you could do to become healthier.
5. Eat healthy snacks like almonds and rice cakes between breakfast, lunch, and dinner and don't eat carbs after 6 p.m. Put all your healthy items at eye level in the pantry. We are programmed to look at the things at eye level first. Easy to do.

So those are five proven easy-to-do things to eat healthier. In Chapter 8, I go into greater detail on the top 10 health decisions, but for now, think about the easy things you can do, because let's face it, our busy lives today are packed with competing priorities. It's filled with all sorts of temptations and distractions, especially with social media. Overwhelm, competing priorities, and temptations can paralyze us from taking action and be disciplined. Overwhelm can keep us in our comfort zone.

Start with one simple, positive change you could make in your life. When you do this, you take advantage of small victories and build momentum to prepare you for your next one.

The problem we all have is making the choice each day to do what we need to do. We can get in our own way. We find a way to justify our excuses. We find reasons not to make the right choice. We find reasons to stay in our comfort zone.

One way to look at making the right choices is to ask yourself two questions:

1. How would you feel at the end of the day if you did the things you planned and said you would do?
2. How would you feel at the end of the day if you didn't follow your plan and do the things you should have done?

We know the answer. So why do we sometimes choose not to do the things we are supposed to do? Why do we find excuses? Because what is easy to do is easy not to do. Our choices have no immediate consequence in the short term. The results of our decisions are not visible in the present. If we knew we would have a heart attack tomorrow for eating that double cheeseburger, would we still stop at that burger joint? If we knew that not showing attention and appreciation to our spouse would result in getting divorced tomorrow, would we come home after a bad day and ignore them and complain about something they did? As they say, time will either promote you or expose you. The problem is that we are human. And humans react irrationally from time to time. Okay, let's be honest. We act irrationally on an almost daily basis. Have you ever made the decision to start being more frugal, watch less TV, or exercise more, only to find yourself buying something you don't need, spending a day binge-watching Netflix, or skipping that gym day just one more time? The rational side of us knows we should do it, but then the impulsive, uncontrollable side of us takes over and causes us to do the exact opposite.

As Jim Rohn often said, "The pain of discipline weighs ounces, while the pain of regret weighs tons." We must all suffer one of two things: the pain of discipline or the pain of regret. It's not that we might have to, or we may have to; it is something we must do. If you don't commit to being disciplined, it will bleed into everything else in your life. If you go to the office and don't do the things you're supposed to, surf the internet, don't follow your plan, etc., you will go home and guess what? You will still be thinking about work and what you could have done. You will not be present. You will not be creating the experience you want with your family to make life more balanced and meaningful. More success will take time. Better health will take time. More meaningful relationships will take time. More time than most are willing to wait. There is no someday. There is only today.

Discipline is about taking the steps each day you need to achieve the things you want to achieve with your life, your health, and your wealth. How do you lose 30 pounds? One pound at a time. How do you save $20,000? One dollar at a time. How do you improve your relationship with your spouse? One conversation at a time. Small disciplines done every day will eventually lead to more wins. Discipline produces results, just not results we can see immediately sometimes. Back to what Jim Rohn said about discipline and regret: you have to pick one. It is more fun to spend than to save, but in the end, you will wish you would have saved. It is more fun to eat an Oreo cookie than it is to go to the gym, but in the end, you will wish you had chosen the gym. It's a choice. It's a choice that sometimes is hard to make because we can always justify to ourselves that we can do it tomorrow.

2.   Lack of Commitment

"Commitment means staying loyal to what you said you were
going to do long after that mood you said it in has left you."
– Inky Johnson

If you can put your goals aside for the wishes of others, you haven't committed to them fully yet. If a buddy says, "do you want to meet for happy hour at 3:00?" and you go without having reached your goals for the day, your commitment level is not there yet. There is no in-between in commitment. Either you do, or you don't. Unless a commitment is made, there is just talk with no plans. Lack of commitment to do what's needed is the single biggest cause of not reaching any goal.

I believe commitment comes from your standards and what you value. If you truly want something, you will commit to it, and it eventually becomes your standard. I will discuss setting new standards for your life, wealth, and health later in the 7 Steps chapter.

3.   Lack of Belief

"Believe in yourself, your abilities, and your potential. Never
let self-doubt hold you captive. You are worthy of all that you
dream of and hope for."
– Roy Bennett

Belief is the thermostat that regulates what we accomplish in life. If you don't have belief, you won't do the things you are capable of. Zig Ziglar was right when he said, "It's impossible to consistently behave in a way that is inconsistent with the way you see yourself." Every aspect of our life is affected by how we see ourselves, our belief in ourselves.

In the book *The Answer* by John Assaraf and Murray Smith, they write about all the negative messages we receive when growing up. By the time we are 17, we have heard the words "no you can't" an average of 150,000 times. During that same period of time we heard the words "yes you can" about 5,000 times. That is a ratio of 30 to 1. Our belief in ourselves, strong or weak, stems back to childhood. The good news is that you can implant new beliefs by focusing on your personal development and by surrounding yourself with people who believe in you. Sometimes you just need someone to believe in you first, before you can believe in yourself. Sometimes, you just need to take action regardless of if you know it's possible for you at this moment.

You may know your next step but can't see a way to do it because you don't believe it is possible. Telling yourself you don't think it's possible will lead to a loss of motivation, as you will stop trying to achieve something you think isn't possible. To help take steps in the right direction, you need to get a clear vision of what you want, believe you can achieve it, and a strong reason for wanting to achieve it. We will dig into this in more detail in the 7 Steps chapter.

The problem with the human mind is that it is divided into two parts, according to Darren Hardy, founder of *Success Magazine.* He calls them the thinker and the prover. He says, "Whatever the mind thinks about, the prover has to prove that thought to be true. If your thinker thinks I am not smart enough or incapable of something, your prover will scan over all your past experiences and pull from it the things that validate and prove that thought right. The prover will look at everything in the present environment or your current situation and reinforce that thought. It will find something in its experience search and the over thinker will say, "See I told you so. I told you I wasn't smart enough or capable," proving the thinker right. What happens now is that you start to act in ways that reinforce this belief and so you become. The prover has won again. Proved you, the over thinker, right. So to stop this cycle, only think about things you want your prover to prove true, and thus it is what you will create."

You need to believe that it's possible, but more importantly, you need to believe it's possible for you. If you want to improve your life – lose weight, earn more money, build and keep more of your wealth, whatever the goal may be – you must first see yourself as worthy and capable of accomplishing your goals.

It has been said that the size of your success is determined by the size of your belief! You're going to earn what you think you're worth. T. Harv Eker says in his book *Secrets of the Millionaire Mind*, "It all comes down to this: if your subconscious 'financial blueprint' is not 'set' for success, nothing you learn, nothing you know, and nothing you do will make much of a difference. Your blueprint for success is like a thermostat. If the temperature in the room is seventy-two degrees, chances are good that the thermostat is set to seventy-two degrees. The only way to permanently change the temperature in the room is to reset the thermostat. In the same way, the only way to change your level of success 'permanently' is to reset your success thermostat."

So don't get too comfortable. Do your best each day. Commit to trying new things, believe in yourself, and get out of your own way.

Wise Life Tip: Read a book like *The Compound Effect* by Darren Hardy, *The Magic of Thinking Big* by David J. Schwartz, or *Atomic Habits* by James Clear to get out of your comfort zone, think bigger, and learn more about how to create lasting habits.

MOMENTOUS DECLARATION #6

I believe I am capable of living a richer life. The amount of my success in life is determined by the amount of my belief.

LIFE DECISION #8: BE CONSISTENT WITH YOUR WORDS AND ACTIONS

"Be Impeccable With Your Word. Speak with integrity. Say only what you mean. Avoid using the word to speak against yourself or to gossip about others. Use the power of your word in the direction of truth and love."

– Don Miguel Ruiz

The fact is our mindset follows our words. What we say to ourselves in our head will reflect the way we project ourselves. Bestselling author and podcast host of "All It Takes Is a Goal," Jon Acuff said, "If we talked to a loved one the way we talk to ourselves, would they be ok with that? Or if you repeated what you said on the inside out loud, would it sound encouraging? We have to give ourselves permission to talk kinder to ourselves. If you wouldn't say it to someone else, you shouldn't say it to yourself, because the way you talk to yourself on the inside is eventually the way you talk to everyone else on the outside."

Be consistent with how you talk to yourself and others. There was a study at MIT that looked at someone being told they couldn't do something. They found that with just that one negative comment, it takes 17 times of someone telling us that "we can" to neutralize that one time of someone telling us we can't. Use encouraging words. For yourself. For others.

Be Consistent with Your Word

I believe being consistent with your word is about following through. If you say something, follow through with action. If you say you're going to do something, do it. When you get in the habit of not following through, you will be known as the talker, and you will not only let yourself down but also let others down. Don't say something unless you can follow up on your words with action.

Don't gossip or talk about others behind their backs. People who talk negatively about other people behind their backs usually have some self-esteem issues. Possibly they need to talk negatively about others to feel better about themselves. Don't be known as a gossiper.

Don't tell lies, even little white ones. I tell my kids all the time that even little lies can come back and bite you one day. You don't want to be known as a person who lies or tells fibs. Being consistent with your word is about being truthful and honest.

Be Consistent with Your Actions

Have you ever made a bad judgment call in your life? Have you ever wondered if you could have done something different or said something different after a meeting with a client or arguing with someone you care about? Have you ever done something you are not proud of? How many bad decisions have you made that you later regretted?

I wrote a song a long time ago called "Jumbotron." I often tell my kids about the Jumbotron effect when they make a bad decision. Basically, the concept is that if the decision you made or the thing you did was displayed on a Jumbotron at a big event for everyone to see, would you be proud of it? Or would you be embarrassed? Think about the words you are about to say, the decisions or actions you are about to make, and whether it would make you proud or embarrassed if 30,000 people saw it on a Jumbotron.

To have a more positive influence on other people, you have to be consistent with what you say and do. Change the things you say to yourself and change the things you say to others. People may not remember everything you say, but they will remember whether it was positive or negative and how it made them feel. Say what you mean and mean what you say. Be consistent with your words and actions.

In the 7 Steps chapter you will learn more about the M.A.D.E. LifePlan and may choose to focus improving your emotional health for you and others. Over 90 days, as part of your M.A.D.E. Life Action Plan, you will focus on ONE MOMENTOUS THING you can do to impact your personal well-being.

LIFE DECISION #9: COMMIT TO PERSONAL GROWTH

"You have to see value in yourself to add value to yourself.
Personal development is the belief that you are worth the effort."
– Dennis Waitley

I like the way Jon Acuff looks at self-development as a new gift to open rather than a problem to fix. I truly believe you are either going through something or you are growing through something. I don't think I would have come through losing my wife in 2017 as strong as I feel like I am without having personal development. Self-development was a gift for me. I am not perfect. I get down every once in a while. I lose my motivation from time to time. I have times when I feel like I am going sideways. Personal growth, like success, is not linear. It sometimes is messy. It looks like the chart of a volatile stock from time to time, but personal growth will help you make progress in an upward trend. You will not be the same person you are right now three years from now or five years from now. You will be stronger and better.

Personal development is an investment in yourself. It helps you find your potential, become more optimistic, focus on what's right, and be more resilient. It helps you strengthen your mindset and overcome limiting beliefs that have held you back. I am who I am today because I committed to personal growth over 15 years ago.

Reading self-books is not for everyone. Some think people who read self-development books are too optimistic, too positive, or quote too much on their Facebook pages. But people who think that do not have a growth mindset. Reading one book won't necessarily change your life, but reading something positive every day will compound over time to help you be on your way to living a more positive life and positivity is contagious.

Personal Development Helps You Invest in Yourself

If you don't think you are worth investing in, then you probably won't put in the time that is needed to grow to your potential. The fact is: you are worth it. There are just too many benefits that personal growth and self-development bring into your life that cannot be ignored. Jim Rohn often said that your success will rarely exceed your personal growth.

You have to be intentional about your personal growth. Once you start being intentional, it will compound over time. It will build upon itself and eventually change the direction of your life. Many people think they can "get by" without it. Many are skeptical if self-development even works. Millions of books have been sold on personal development, and if it works, wouldn't you think millions of people would be more successful than they are? Of course. But because we are all human, just reading books won't make us more successful. We have to take action. I believe personal development gives you the tools to become more successful:

If you are skeptical about personal growth, here are some numbers based on research done by the International Coach Federation.

- 62.4% of people focused on self-development got smarter with goal-setting.
- 60.5% of people focused on self-development received a more balanced life.
- 57.1% of people focused on self-development experienced lower stress.
- 52.4% of people focused on self-development became more self-confident.
- 33.8% of people focused on self-development became healthier and fitter.
- 33.3% of people focused on self-development enriched their relationship with their family.

You may be asking yourself, why aren't the numbers higher? Why isn't it 70%, 90%, or even 100% improvement in people? The only simple answer comes down to action. Some will take it and some won't. Some will read a book and take some action, and some will read a book and hope that, just by reading it, things will improve. That is why people are still buying self-development books, and the industry is thriving. People are looking for the wisdom to change their lives. The wisdom of the world is available, as Jim Rohn would say. You have to find the messages that will resonate with you. You can read a book today and three years later pick it up and read it again, and it will have three times the impact. It will be like reading it for the first time, picking out information, concepts, and wisdom you didn't see before. Why? Because three years from now, if you commit to personal growth, you will be drastically different from how you are right now.

Personal Development Helps You Find Your Potential

Your success will only grow to the extent that you do. Many of us could sleepwalk through our professional and personal lives, but is that really what you want to do with your career? Your life? Sleepwalk? Do you want to go through life just getting by and nothing more, or do you want to live a richer life? You wouldn't have made it this far reading this book if you were one of those individuals. You want something greater for yourself. For your family. For your future.

Personal growth and self-development make you self-aware. You get to know who you are differently. It makes you aware of your beliefs and values and helps you design a life based on who you are and want to be. Personal growth and self-development also give you clarity. It is your guide to help you avoid distractions that don't contribute to your vision. It will give you a sense of direction. Once you have become clear on what you want out of life, you will have a strong force pulling you in the direction you need to go. You will have a sense that you are moving in the right direction and only choose things that are worthy of your time and that help you make progress on your vision.

Take a look at your schedule over the next 90 days. How much time is dedicated to personal growth? You can be intentional about your growth. If you want to do great things with your life, you have to grow.

Personal Development Helps You Become an Optimist

> *"It takes no courage to be a pessimist, to believe it's not going to work or to find what is wrong."*
>
> – Tony Robbins

Would you consider yourself a realist or an optimist? I always used to think that an optimist always thinks positively. I used to tell people I was a realist because I didn't view myself as overly optimistic the majority of the time. When it comes down to it, being an optimist all the time is physiologically impossible. No one can walk around with a ray of sunshine always on them like a spotlight. An optimist is simply someone who knows how to intercept, redirect, and stop negative thoughts before they occur. They turn negative thoughts into positive thoughts. It sounds a little bit like what meditation helps you with – redirecting thoughts. You don't necessarily have to change how you think, just change what you think about. It is much easier to say, "I'm an optimist," when you look at optimism this way.

Personal Development Helps You Find What's Right, Not What's Wrong

It's always easy to find what is wrong. Our habit of being positive will shape our lives and determine who we become, as well as how things turn out for us. We need to train ourselves to find the good. Negative thoughts serve no purpose and don't benefit us in any way. It's important to protect our minds from negativity. Some days are easier than others, but it is all about being intentional about trying to be more positive.

People who are most stressed in life are the ones who go to the negative right away and then focus on it without redirecting it to something positive. It is not about not having negative thoughts; it's about the same thing meditation trains you to do with your thoughts. It's about being aware of them and redirecting them. So, if automatic negative thoughts are the first thoughts we have, how do we stop them? We have to offer our mind another choice.

Personal Development Helps You Work on Your Mindset

When was the last time you worked on your mindset? The last time you were aware of your thoughts and redirected them? We spend time building the muscles in our body but very little time building the muscles in our minds. We have automatic thoughts that come up frequently, and most of them are negative. Unfortunately, negativity is already hardwired in our brains. When was the last time you received an unexpected phone call and immediately assumed the worst? This is not uncommon because the brain in our head is simply hardwired to be more sensitive to negative things. The mind will automatically go to the negative of a situation, unless you learn to work on your mindset.

One of the best ways to change your outlook on life is to commit to personal development and growth. At the end of this book is a complete list of the books I have read over the years that have helped me grow into the person I am today.

In the 7 Steps chapter you will learn more about the M.A.D.E. LifePlan and may choose to focus on personal growth. Over 90 days as part of your M.A.D.E. Life Action Plan, you will focus on One Momentous Thing you can every day to grow and improve.

Wise Life Tip: Buy one personal development book that can help you in your current situation. Read it, take notes and apply one thing to your life. Some of my favorites are:

1. *The Magic of Thinking Big* by David Schwartz.
2. *The 12-Week Year* by Brian Moran.
3. *What Got You Here Won't Get You There* by Marshall Goldsmith.

MOMENTOUS DECLARATION #7

I am committed to personal growth because my wealth and success will only grow to the extent that I grow.

LIFE DECISION #10: DON'T STRESS OUT ABOUT THINGS YOU CAN'T CONTROL

We spend a lot of time worrying about things that never even happen. We all know there are things in life that we can't control. Worrying about them stresses us out. Instead of focusing on what we can't control, we need to find a way to put our energy into what we can control. Find solutions to the problems we can solve. What we have complete control over is our thoughts. In his book *As a Man Thinketh*, James Allen makes the simple but bold statement that "Good thoughts and actions can never produce bad results; bad thoughts and actions can never produce a good result." Good results in your life will only come from your frame of mind. The more responsibility you accept for the things in your life, the more control you will feel you have. The greater control you feel you have, the more confident you become. The happier you become. When you feel in control of your life, you will set more goals for yourself. You will also have the determination to achieve the ones most important to you.

We can't always control what happens to us, but we can control how we react. The difference between people who struggle and those who thrive is how they face their problems. The most successful people don't let their circumstances or situations get the best of them. They don't let their past get in the way. It's been said that it is our decisions, not our circumstances, that control how our life turns out. With the right mindset, you can overcome almost any obstacle or problem. Believe in your ability to figure things out.

We have all heard the expression, "This too will pass." Even saying this expression over and over during a tough time in your life seems to be so far from the truth when you are in it. It feels for what seems like forever that it will never pass, but it does. I know during the first year after my wife died, the grief felt like it would never go away. Although it never went away, it did get less and less intense. When you do have tough times, I find it extremely helpful to find an outlet. Make a gratitude journal, draw, paint, or read a motivational book. For me, I always turn to writing songs. Getting my thoughts on a page, negative or positive, allows me to be grateful for the good and, more importantly, release the bad from my mind. Many of the songs I wrote with feelings of hurt or pain just got thrown in a cardboard box of the past. These songs, although not necessarily uplifting, always serve as a reminder of the things I endured and became stronger because of them.

Minimize Your Worries

If you have worry or fear pop up when you try something new, are ruminating on something, or preparing to make a significant change, try using Dale Carnegie's Magic Formula for Solving Worry Situations. It's a process to create a calm detachment from your worries and find a little peace.

Step 1 – Analyze the Problem.

The first step is to analyze our problem honestly. Start by writing down what worries you, even if it feels too personal or private – this is for your eyes only. Whatever it is, write it down.

Continue writing down everything that is cluttering your mind at the moment. The key here is not only to clear your mind of each worry but to write out the worst possible outcome. What is the worst thing that could happen?

Step 2 – Accept the Worst Possible Outcome.

After you have written down each worry and each worst possible outcome, the next thing you do is accept that the worst may happen. You must accept the worst-case scenario so that you can relax. When your mind is distracted by fear, you will find it really hard to focus.

Take a few moments to consider each problem in the first step of this exercise and write down how you will accept it. You will feel relief in your body as you do this.

Step 3 – Minimize the Problem.

In the final part of this exercise, take the time to figure out how you can improve upon your worst outcome. This step is where you will "minimize the problem," as Carnegie says. You will concentrate on the future, toss out all the what-ifs, blame, and shame. For this next step, you need to ask yourself, how can I minimize these consequences?

Some problems are hard to minimize, but when you take the steps to analyze them and see the worst that can happen, you can find a way to minimize the problems in your head and give yourself a little more control and peace of mind.

Are Feelings Creating Our Problems?

Some people wake up in the morning and the first thing they do is think about their problems. Every one of those problems has an emotion associated with it and all of a sudden they start feeling unhappy. According to Joe Dispenza, "our thoughts talk to our brain, and our feelings talk to our body. When these thoughts lean to the negative or are linked to a painful past, it affects the way we move and act in the present. And this impacts our future and who we are becoming." Try journaling about your problems. Get them off your chest and go to bed at night a little clearer so you can wake up with a mind ready for a better day.

If you focus on what you can control rather than what you can't, you will be on your way to living a richer life with less stress and less worry.

> **Wise Life Tip**: If you are stressed out or anxious about something, take a walk or simply close your eyes and take five long, deep breathes: eight seconds breathing in and eight seconds breathing out. If that doesn't work, listen to the song "Worry No More" by Amos Lee and crank it up. That song always makes me feel better when I am worrying too much.

Summary of Life Decisions to Live a Richer Life

Life is a game, and it comes down to how you play it. Most of us are just going through life on autopilot with no plan to grow and improve.

Here is an example of a plan to become better at life over your first year:

First 90-Day Period:

1. Take time to write out all your reasons for wanting better health, more wealth, and a richer life.

2. Read a positive book like *Attitude is Everything*.
3. Practice the three As every day with someone you care about.

Second 90-Day Period:

1. Become aware of the things you say to yourself and find more empowering positive messages.
2. Plan a unique experience.
3. Try the gratitude experiment where you don't complain for 24 hours. Then practice gratitude for seven days. Then try doing it every day.

Third 90-Day Period:

1. Listen to positive mindset podcasts for 15 minutes every day.
2. Plan some volunteer work, or give to a cause you care about.
3. Take a bucket list trip.

Fourth 90-Day Period:

1. Read a good book on being intentional, like *The Power of Intention* by Dr. Wayne Dyer.
2. Step out of your comfort zone and try something new.
3. Try the Three Moments of Joy journaling exercise for 30 days.

One year from now, you will have created a more intentional life, which will become your new standard. You will feel better, be more fulfilled, and have more meaning. You will be more positive, more grateful, and have stronger, richer relationships with those you care about. Reflect on some of these life decisions and ask yourself which ones resonate with you the most. Deciding what you want to improve in your life will help you develop a more meaningful M.A.D.E. 90-Day Life Action Plan in the 7 Steps chapter of this book.

CHAPTER FIVE

WEALTH DECISIONS FOR A RICHER LIFE

I've been studying the markets since I was 18 and have been working in the financial services industry for over 25 years. Throughout my experience, I've learned many valuable lessons, but the first six of the following 10 Wealth Decisions impacted my wealth the most. Buying stocks on margin was my hardest lesson. These 10 Wealth Decisions can help you establish a foundation for a richer life for you and your family. Beyond these 10, other important wealth decisions are getting out of debt, paying off your mortgage, and investing in a Health Savings Account (HSA) account, which I will discuss in the Wealth Decisions Plan to Achieve Financial Freedom in Chapter 6.

One of my biggest financial regrets was not living within my means sooner in life. I had a lot of fun, but at the expense of my future. The sooner you can find a way to live within your means, the more chances you will have to create a plan for your future and let the power of compounding work for you.

There is a difference between money and wealth. We sometimes ask ourselves, "How do we get more money?" Except this may be the wrong question. The question should be, "How do I create and keep more of my wealth for me and my family?" Many of us grew up thinking money was fixed and there was only so much to go around. Money is not wealth. Money is a medium of exchange. Money might be somewhat fixed for most people in terms of their income, but wealth is not. You can always create more wealth. If you fix up a house, you have created wealth. If you invest your money for the long term in the stock market, you will create more wealth over time. We all have the opportunity to create more wealth for ourselves. Wealth equals choice and freedom. Creating and keeping more of your wealth over time requires living by some proven principles and making decisions in the best interest of your future. The following wealth decisions can help you do just that.

WEALTH DECISION #1: LIVE WITHIN YOUR MEANS

We often feel the pressure to keep up with our friends and neighbors, especially when it comes to wanting shiny new objects. A rich life is not just about nice things, although ads getting us to want this or that would lead us to believe that. We can find a balance between a fulfilling life and saving for the future by being clear on what truly matters to us both now and in the long run.

I grew up with a father who preached about living within your means constantly and lived by example. Unfortunately, when he said it to me, it usually went in one ear and out the other. My dad lived well below his means and was very frugal and found ways to save any way he could. I grew up with an older brother and had a lot of hand-me-downs. I remember when I was on the Grant Photography Hockey team when I was young, we wore red and white uniforms, and I had a blue Pro-Tec helmet that was handed down from my brother. Everyone else had red, white, or black helmets. I guess the one advantage was that my dad could spot me on the ice so he could yell, "Hustle, hustle, hustle!"

When I was in high school, I played tennis and soccer. This was the era of Andre Agassi, so naturally I sported a mullet and a pretty good one I might say. Andre used to be in a commercial for the Canon Rebel camera and he always ended the commercial by saying, "Image is Everything." My dad always gave me a hard time back then and would say things like, "All you care about is what you look like." He was disappointed when I spent my first paycheck from the County Seat on some $70 Girbaud Jeans and a $50 B.U.M. Equipment sweatshirt. I also bought the newest Andre Agassi Nike shoes and gear so I could play "Rock & Roll" tennis just like Andre. I might not have won a lot of matches playing first singles for North High, but I looked good. It turns out, though, that image is not everything.

Later, after high school, I went through a polo phase. I think at one point, I owned 10 branded polo shirts at $80 bucks a pop. My dad always said, "Why would you ever pay $80 for a polo shirt when you can buy one at K-Mart for $12?" My justification was that they lasted a lot longer and didn't shrink.

When I started in the financial services industry, I bought some fancy suits and ties and even bought some skinny leather suspenders so I looked like a stockbroker (hope those never come back in style, or maybe they never were). I wanted to look my best even if I couldn't afford those nice suits. I felt like I needed to look successful even before I was. When you are surrounded by other successful advisors, you tend to want to be like them. I went on trips I couldn't afford, bought a nice car I certainly had no business buying, and wasn't afraid to spend 100+ dollars at a fancy steak restaurant. I liked nice things then and I like nice things now, but I have learned through the years that experiences are more important than things and the only way to have enough money to build wealth was to live within my means rather than above it. It wasn't until I got laid off from a job as a mutual fund wholesaler that I changed my spending to start living below my means. I had to. I was unemployed, had a BMW X5, and a townhome mortgage that was too much for me. My brother moved in to help with the mortgage, I sold my BMW X5 and bought a used Nissan Xterra with no power windows or power locks. I was forced to lower the cost of my lifestyle and live below my means. I didn't have a choice. As my dad always said, "Brian, you always find a way to land on your feet." Eventually I started back at the brokerage firm I left and built up a successful office, but started to think about my own vision for what I wanted things to look like for myself and my clients. In 2021, I made the decision to go independent to have more control over how I served my clients as a fiduciary advisor. Today I own my own firm, on my terms, and feel like I am living a more balanced and purpose-driven life.

Creating a Budget to Live Within Your Means

There is all kinds of advice about budgeting out there, but a good rule of thumb to create financial freedom when managing your finances is to limit your debt expenses (mortgage, car payments, other debt) to 35% of your net income, allocating 25% of your income toward fulfilling your basic needs, 15% toward having new experiences, and 25% toward savings to ensure financial independence or freedom. Look at where you are spending money. Don't buy things you don't need. Stop buying a latte at Starbucks every day. Spend money on experiences rather than things. You can't create financial independence or freedom without first living within your means. As my dad would say, if you make a good income and are successful, you better have something to show for it other than fancy things. Living within your means is the first step on your journey to build more wealth and have something to show for your income and success.

> **Wise Wealth Tip**: Look at your budget and where you are spending money. Get rid of subscriptions you don't need or stop eating out as much. Most people can find $200–300 of unnecessary expenses they can do without.

To access the financial freedom calculator, go to: https://www.momentous wealthadvisors.com/tools.

WEALTH DECISION #2: PAY YOURSELF FIRST

Most individuals pay their bills and then invest if there is anything left over. A better wealth decision is to pay yourself first by putting a percentage of money away before you pay your bills. Paying yourself first is how my dad retired at 50. Most Americans do the exact opposite. A good goal to shoot for is to put away at least 20% first, and then pay your bills with the rest. If you can't afford to put away 20% right now, start with 5% or 10% and find a way to work toward putting away 15–20%.

I might have had a lot of hand-me-downs as a kid or lived above my means for the first five years of my career as an advisor, but I am glad I had a father who preached the pay-yourself-first philosophy to us early in life. I would not be in the position I am in today without adopting this mindset. He has been retired for almost 30 years, and my dad and mom live in Arizona for half the year and Minnesota for the other half because he adopted this philosophy early in life. He is still frugal; that hasn't changed. As he would say, "He has lived a good life." Paying yourself first can set you up to achieve a richer life in the future. Five years from now, 10 years from now, 20 years from now, 30 years from now, you will be glad you did.

I believe there are three things you can have regarding your future finances.

1. Financial Security
2. Financial Independence
3. Financial Freedom

At first glance, those three things all look similar, but they are very different. All three are desirable goals and can be achieved with a well-thought-out plan.

1. **Financial Security** will give you just that. You will feel secure enough to retire, but won't be able to do all the things you want to do in retirement.
2. **Financial Independence** allows you to do more of the things you want whether traveling, or helping the kids or grandkids with college, and gives you a nice margin of confidence not to have to worry.
3. **Financial Freedom** is about having more choices. More chances to achieve your bigger dreams. More options to take trips you never thought you could afford. More money to leave a legacy if so desired.

The 35-20-10 Rule

Whatever you want your ideal life to be, paying yourself first is a crucial discipline you need to focus on. The 35-20-10 Rule is simply the percentage you put away of your income and whether that percentage is enough to achieve your goal of financial security, financial independence, or financial freedom. Everyone has different lifestyles, budgets, and dreams. If you want financial freedom, putting away between 30 and 40% may be what you need to do to achieve that goal. If you desire financial independence, setting aside 20% of your income may be necessary to achieve that feeling of independence. If you want to create financial security, 10% is what you may need to achieve security. Whatever your goals are, you can develop a plan to help you achieve your desired lifestyle.

Always remember that part of paying yourself first should be having money go into an emergency fund. You should aim to have at least six months of after-tax expenses in an emergency fund. So, if you need $7,000 after tax each month to live comfortably, you should have a minimum of $42,000 saved for emergencies.

Momentous Milestones

People often ask me how much they should have saved at their particular age. This is a big question, and the answer is different for everyone. But there is a path you need to be on if you want to achieve financial independence or financial freedom.

Your Thirties

In your thirties, you may juggle various responsibilities, such as starting a family, buying a home, or advancing your career. It's crucial in your thirties to start to balance short-term goals and long-term financial planning. Review your budget regularly to accommodate new expenses and ensure you save for short- and long-term goals. Evaluate your insurance coverage and purchase life insurance to cover debts like your mortgage and your income for a period of time. If you have started a family, insurance is even more important. You may want to cover college expenses and the costs associated with raising children. Have a financial advisor run an insurance needs analysis to evaluate appropriate insurance coverage. During your thirties, your goals should be to increase your retirement contributions each year so that you can start to take advantage of the time value of money and compounding interest. Paying yourself first can set up a great foundation on which to build and get you in the habit of prioritizing your financial future. When you are in your forties and fifties, you will be glad you started saving in your thirties. As a general rule of thumb, you should be surpassing your first 100k in retirement savings when you are in your early thirties on your way to having 200–250k late in your thirties.

Your Forties

Everyone is on different career paths, but you should be in your prime earnings years, saving the maximum in your work plan, and contributing to Roth IRAs or Backdoor Roth IRAs if you are over the income limits. As a general rule of thumb, you should have saved at least three times your salary toward retirement. For example, if you make 150k, you should have about 450k in retirement accounts. If you are not there yet, it's not too late to get on track.

Your Fifties

As retirement draws nearer, your fifties are a critical time for financial planning. Assess your readiness to retire on your terms by reviewing your savings, investments, and projected retirement income. Consider consulting with a financial advisor to fine-tune your plan and make any needed adjustments.

These are considered your high-income and savings years. As a general rule of thumb, you should have six times your current salary saved for retirement. For example, if you make 150k/year, you should have close to 900k saved. If you are not there yet, you can now save more in your work plans and your IRA accounts using catch-up contributions.

If you are in your thirties, forties, or fifties and have not saved as much as you should have, don't get discouraged. It is never too late to start saving for the future.

So let's look at what starting from scratch looks like by showing what each of the three Fs look like over 25 years. Here is an example of the power of paying yourself first: a 40-year-old couple with nothing saved yet for the future earns a joint income of $200,000 per year and invest different percentages based on their goals. We assume an 8% rate of return and a 4% withdrawal rate at retirement. The incomes in retirement in these examples are before tax for simplicity.

Financial Security (10%)

$20k saved per year ($1,666/month) = approx. $1.4 million at age 65.
Potential Financial Security Income = $4,500/month.

Financial Independence (20%)

$40k saved per year ($3,333/month) = approx. $2.9 million at age 65.
Potential Financial Independence Income = $9,500/month.

Financial Freedom (35%)

$70k saved per year ($5,833/month) = approx. $5 million at age 65.
Potential Financial Freedom Income = $200k/year or $16,500/month.
To access the financial freedom calculator, go to: https://www.momentous
wealthadvisors.com/tools.

Paying yourself first will allow you to create wealth and have your money one day working harder than you do. One day, your investment portfolio will make more in a day than you make in three months of working. That is the power of paying yourself first and investing for the long term.

In the 7 Steps chapter you will learn more about the M.A.D.E. LifePlan and will define what you want to accomplish with your wealth in the short and long term. You will create a 10-year vision and a plan to achieve what is most important to you when it comes to your financial situation. Over 90 days as part of your M.A.D.E. Life Action Plan, you will focus on ONE MOMENTOUS THING you can do each month to build and keep your wealth.

Wise Wealth Tip: Look at last year's federal taxes. Whatever that amount was, try to save that amount this year if you can afford it and want to achieve financial freedom. Why should the government be a bigger beneficiary of your success than you?

WEALTH DECISION #3: INVEST IN HIGH-QUALITY STOCKS

Early in my investing life, I always tried to find the next Amazon, Netflix, or Microsoft. I found stocks that did well in the short term, chased momentum growth stocks, and invested in smaller companies thinking I was smarter than the rest of the market. If I had a process for investing in companies like I do today, my success would have been substantially greater. Hindsight is 20/20 but investing in quality stocks with favorable risk/reward, solid fundamentals, competitive moats, and strong management would have been much more profitable over time than investing in small start-ups with no earnings or companies that were the "stock of the day."

Investing in high-quality stocks is smart because they represent financially stable and successful companies with a proven track record of profitability and growth. These companies have a strong brand image, efficient management, innovative products, and a loyal customer base. Investing in high-quality companies increases the likelihood of receiving consistent and growing dividends, long-term capital appreciation, and a relatively low risk of losses if you invest for the long term. Also, high-quality stocks tend to perform better than low-quality stocks during market downturns, making them a more reliable investment option for all types of market environments.

The key to investing in stocks is to have a process. There are over 20,000 individual stocks listed on the exchanges around the world, and there are close to 8,000 in the United States alone. Stock investing takes discipline. A structured and strategic process for picking stocks is crucial for successful investing. I use a process I developed and have refined over the years called the Momentous P.R.U.D.E.N.T. Process. It starts with an advanced screen using an underutilized rule called the "Rule of 40." The Rule of 40 is adding the revenue growth rate and the net profit margin of a company and if that number is 40 or higher, then it passes the test. We then screen for high earnings growth, low debt, and attractive prices to identify potential stocks to buy.

For more information on the Momentous P.R.U.D.E.N.T. Process for picking stocks go to: https://www.momentouswealthadvisors.com/stock-investing.

Note: I believe most individuals should start by building a solid base of investments in their retirement accounts in low-cost mutual funds and ETFs before investing in individual stocks outside their retirement plans. Individual stocks are appropriate for individuals who have at least $50,000 saved in a taxable account and have six months of expenses saved in an emergency account. My general rule of thumb for investing in individual stocks is if you can't buy at least 10 stocks to diversify your money in different industries, you should stick with low-cost ETFs or mutual funds.

Wise Wealth Tip: If you don't have $50k saved, but want to own individual stocks, buy 10 high-quality stocks in different industries using a dollar cost averaging program to take advantage of volatility.

My Hardest Financial Lesson

If you decide to buy stocks to build your wealth, avoid using leverage to enhance your returns. Investing with borrowed money or buying on margin is one of the greatest ways to multiply your returns by two or three times but also a good way to multiply your losses by two or three times. I learned this valuable lesson early in my investing life, along with many others in the tech boom and subsequent bust from 1999 to 2000. At the time, I was a new financial advisor and had about $20,000 saved in a taxable investment account loaded with profitable tech stocks and some not-so-profitable dot.com stocks. At the time, the maintenance margin requirement was about 35%, which meant I could invest another $37,000 on margin making my total portfolio invested worth around $57,000 ($20,000 was my own money and the rest was borrowed with my stocks as collateral). The problem is that if you use all your borrowing power to buy more stocks on margin and your stocks go down, you will get a margin call if your margin percentage drops below 35%. This means you either have to sell stocks to cover the margin call or come up with cash.

Well, in late 1999, I kept buying more tech stocks like everyone else. The difference was that every time they went up and I had more buying power, I would borrow more money to buy more tech stocks. But what goes up must come down. The last stock I bought was in a small company called Microstrategy, which is well-known today for its sizable stake in Bitcoin. I bought it for about $102 per share right before a vacation to Mexico in early March 2000. Five days later, I finally was able to get a newspaper. In 2000 we didn't have instant access to stock quotes like we do today. The quote was around $320 per share. I bought 250 shares and made over $50k in six days. Needless to say, drinks were on me that night. Two days later, Microstrategy went from $320 per share down to about $180 per share and then went down to about $100 per share in the matter of a week. All tech stocks started crumbling, and my almost $220,000 portfolio started crumbling with it. Margin call after margin call, I had to sell stocks to cover each margin call. Instead of selling more than required, I sold just enough each time to meet the call hoping that stocks would start to bottom and recover. They never did. Many tech stocks during that period fell more than 70%. At the end, my portfolio was worth less than my original investment of $20,000.

This was a very painful lesson to learn, but I am just glad I learned it when I was young. I still use margin from time to time, but mostly to fund something I can pay off in three to six months and never more than 10% of my collateral.

Leverage is powerful on the way up, but on the way down it's like a falling knife. Leverage is what caused the financial crisis of 2008–2009 and many other crises we have had in the financial markets over the years. It seems like even Wall Street and the banking industry never learn. Banks and big brokerage firms were sometimes leveraged 10 to 1 on CMOs (Collateralized Mortgage Obligations) in 2008, meaning for every $100k in CMOs, they were borrowing 10 times that to buy more. Does that sound smart to you? That is why Merrill Lynch is now a Bank of America company. They were so leveraged that it almost brought down the most well-known brokerage firm. Lehman Brothers wasn't so lucky. They went under on 15 September 2008.

> **Wise Wealth Tip**: Leverage is not your way to create wealth. It is the great destroyer of wealth. Don't borrow money to buy stocks. If you do, never borrow more than 10% of your collateral, and make sure the base of the stocks you are borrowing against are solid blue-chip companies, and not all in one sector.

WEALTH DECISION #4: TAKE ADVANTAGE OF ROTH IRAS AND ROTH 401K OPTIONS

Many individuals make too much money to contribute to Roth IRAs, because of the income limits imposed on eligibility. What many don't know is that there is a strategy called the Back-Door Roth IRA that allows anyone to contribute to a Roth IRA without income limits. It simply involves contributing to a nondeductible IRA and converting it to a Roth IRA the next day. The younger you are, the more powerful investing in a Roth IRA becomes. One disclaimer: if you have an IRA currently, be aware of how Roth conversions work differently when you have an existing IRA account. Consult with a qualified advisor before choosing to start a Back-Door Roth IRA.

It is also important to take advantage of the Roth 401k option if it is available at your current employer. The more money you can accumulate in

Roth accounts, the more tax control you will have when you want to retire. Consult a financial advisor to determine how much you should contribute to pre-tax versus Roth options. Some employers also give employees the ability to defer money into an after-tax plan in addition to their pre-tax deferrals, which you can convert to a Roth IRA at the end of each year. Ask your employer if they have this after-tax option.

If you put $6,000 in a Roth IRA every year starting at age 30 and earn a 10% average rate of return, by the time you are 65, you could have accumulated over $1.5 million, all of which comes out tax-free. Assuming you are in the 28% tax bracket in retirement, you would have to accumulate $2.1 million in an IRA to have the same after-tax benefit.

Wise Wealth Tip: Be more aggressive with your Roth IRA money. The more you accumulate in Roth IRAs, the more tax-free income you will have when you retire.

WEALTH DECISION #5: INVEST SYSTEMATICALLY BY DOLLAR COST AVERAGING

Stock market corrections (−10% or more) occur about once every 1.6 years, and bear markets (−20% or more) occur on average every four years. Since the 1950s, the S&P 500 has experienced around 38 market corrections and 12 bear markets, including the 1990 bear market, when the benchmark index fell 19.9%.

If you systematically invest a set amount per month, which is referred to as dollar cost averaging, you benefit from volatility. During corrections or bear markets, you can buy quality stocks for sometimes 20–40% less. The way dollar cost averaging works is simple. Let's say you are buying a Large Cap Growth ETF that is $10 per share and investing $1,000 per month. That means you could buy 100 shares. If in month two it is worth $12 per share, you can only buy 83.33 shares, which means you are buying fewer shares at a high. If in month four the ETF is now worth $8 per share, you can buy 125 shares with your $1,000, which means you are buying more shares at a low. What do you do when you go into Costco and toothpaste is 40% off? You buy more, right? That same philosophy should apply to how you invest, and dollar cost averaging does that automatically for you.

Warren Buffet's most famous quote, "Be greedy when others are fearful, and be fearful when others are greedy," is easier said than done but easier when you are dollar cost averaging because you are not trying to time the market, just making a wise wealth decision by investing monthly to take advantage of the ups and downs.

Wise Wealth Tip: If the market is going down, increase your contributions by 1.5 x 3 times your current amount if possible. For example, if you are contributing 10% currently, up your contribution to a minimum of 15% during a correction or bear market. Market corrections or bear markets eventually pass, and the more you take advantage of them, the more wealth you will build over time.

WEALTH DECISION #6: DON'T JUST INVEST IN YOUR 401K

If all your money is in a traditional 401k, every dime you take out when you retire will be taxable. We don't know where tax rates will be 10 or 20 years from now, so having all your money in a tax-deferred account doesn't give you much control. It is crucial to have not just investment diversification but also account diversification. Account diversification gives you more flexibility and tax control.

In addition to investing in your 401k and Roth IRAs, you should invest in a taxable account in high-quality stocks or low-cost ETFs. Taxable accounts will give you more control over when you pay taxes and are taxed at more favorable rates, especially if you have long-term capital gains, which are taxed at 0%, 15%, or 20% depending on your tax bracket. Most individuals pay 15% on long-term capital gains.

Your goal should be to put away 25% of your income: 15% in 401ks and Roth IRAs and 10% in a taxable account. Saving money in a taxable account is also crucial if you plan on retiring before age 59½ because 401ks cannot be touched without penalty and taxes until you reach that age. There is an exception to this rule called Rule 72(t), which allows you to start taking money from your IRA or 401k at age 55 without penalty but it requires substantially equal payments over a minimum of five years or until you reach 59½, whichever is longer. Although you are not subject to the 10% early withdrawal penalty, you still have to pay taxes on your distributions.

Wise Wealth Tip: If you want to retire at 55, aim to have at least five times your yearly expenses saved in a taxable account. So if your expenses are $70k after tax per year, your goal would be to have $350,000 in a taxable investment account.

WEALTH DECISION #7:
BE FRUGAL WITH WINDFALLS

Inheriting a significant sum of money can be a life-changing event, but it's important to approach it with a frugal mindset to ensure long-term financial security. The statistics show that it takes people who inherit money about 18 months to spend it all. Don't be a statistic. It's essential to avoid impulsive spending and consider the most prudent and responsible ways to use this potentially life-changing windfall. A windfall doesn't have to be just an inheritance, it could also be a settlement or a large bonus you get from your job. Anything that could potentially change your future financial situation if you invest it wisely.

When it comes to receiving an inheritance, I always ask clients, "How long would it take to save the amount of money you are inheriting?" For example, how long would it take you to save $500,000? Let's say you could put away $2,000 per month, it would take you about 20 years to save $500k. If you saved for 20 years and accumulated $500,000, would you still spend the money the same way as the windfall you are inheriting? Inheriting money can change your life. If you instead invested that $500,000, assuming an 8% return over 20 years, you could accumulate over $2.6 million. Now, that is life-changing.

RULE OF 72: a quick, useful formula that is popularly used to estimate the number of years required to double your invested money at a given annual rate of return is:

$$t \approx \frac{72}{r}$$

For example, at a 10% return, your money would double every 7.2 years. So $500k would be worth $1 million in seven years and would have doubled to $2 million in year 14.

There are three steps I run clients through on what I call the Inheritance Decision Process.

Step 1: Calculate how long it would take you to save the amount you are inheriting.

Step 2: Show the impact of your windfall long-term if you invested it wisely.

You can change your future wealth picture for you and your family. One strategy would be to invest your inheritance and use the dividends to improve your home or take an extra vacation.

Step 3: Visualize scenarios of spending inheritance vs. investing.

Visualize how different your life would be if you invested your inheritance vs. if you spent it unwisely. An inheritance can be life-changing. What would your parents or grandparents want for you?

Here are six things to keep in mind when receiving a windfall:

1. Take time to reflect

Before making any decisions, take the time to reflect on this new wealth. Try to avoid impulsive spending and instead consider the most prudent and responsible ways to use the inheritance.

For example, if you invested a $500,000 inheritance assuming an 8% return over 20 years, you could accumulate over $2.6 million.

2. Seek professional advice

Consulting with financial advisors, estate planners, and tax professionals can provide invaluable insights into how to maximize the inheritance while minimizing tax implications. A well-thought-out financial plan can help safeguard and grow wealth for the future.

3. Establish clear financial goals

Having a clear vision of your financial goals will guide your decision-making process. Whether it's paying off debts, investing for the future, or saving for a major purchase, setting specific goals can help you invest the inheritance wisely.

4. Avoid lifestyle inflation

While it may be tempting to upgrade your lifestyle when you receive an inheritance, resist the urge to increase your lifestyle. Maintaining a frugal mindset and living within your means can help you preserve your inheritance and build more wealth for you and your family.

5. Build a diversified portfolio

Consider investing a big portion of your inheritance in a diverse portfolio to generate long-term returns. A well-thought-out investment strategy in dividend-producing investments can help the inheritance grow over time while only using the income generated from your portfolio for things you may want in the short term. If you don't have things you want to use the dividend income for, reinvest the dividends to build even more wealth for the future.

6.   Philanthropy and legacy planning

If giving back to the community is important to you, consider allocating a portion of the inheritance to charitable causes. Develop a financial plan that includes a legacy plan to ensure that your wealth has a lasting impact on future generations if that is important to you.

> **Wise Wealth Tip**: Invest your inheritance in dividend-producing ETFs and use the dividends without touching the principal to save for that new kitchen remodel, new vehicle, or vacation. Your deceased loved one would want you to enjoy your inheritance, but not waste it. For example, if you inherited $500,000 and could get an average of 3% in dividends, you could take your dividends in cash each quarter and accumulate $15k/year in dividend income that could be used for all the things on your list without touching your original inheritance amount.

You can get more information at www.momentouswealthadvisors.com/inheritance-advice.

WEALTH DECISION #8: NEVER TRY TO TIME THE MARKET

If you ever panic and get out of the market, you will always find a reason not to get back in. It is impossible to time the market. You have to be right twice. You have to get out at the right time (near a high) and get back in at the right time (near a low). Most individuals who get out of the market get out at the bottom and then get back when it feels good to invest again, which is usually after most of the recovery has happened.

In February 2023, Hartford Mutual Funds put out a report called "Timing the Market is Impossible." The report looked at missing the market's best days from 1993 to 2022 versus staying fully invested. If you invested $10,000 in 1993, your $10,000 would be worth over $158,000 by the end of 2022 if invested in the S&P 500. If you missed the 10 best days, it would be worth less than $73,000 (54% less), and if you missed the 50 best days, it would be worth less than $27,000 (83% less).

But what was most interesting about this report was when the best 50 days occurred. The study concluded that:

- 52% of the best 50 days happened during a bear market (or bad market).
- 26% of the best 50 days happened during the first two months of a bull market (when not many think we are in a good market yet).
- 22% of the best 50 days happened during the rest of the bull market (or a good market).

So, over 78% of the best days in the market over the past 30 years happened during what was perceived to be the worst of times.

A good advisor can coach you during difficult periods to ensure you don't succumb to fear or panic and sell during the worst of times. I believe this is the true value of a financial advisor.

Navigating Market Declines

Whether you're a novice just starting your investment journey or a veteran investor, understanding how to handle market corrections is crucial for your long-term success. The most important thing to note is that market corrections are normal. They're part of a healthy market.

Corrections and bear markets are different. They're both a little unnerving, but corrections are generally less severe, and they're shorter-lived than a bear market. Understanding this can help prevent you from making an emotional decision during a small correction. Corrections often coincide with different phases of the economic cycle, and understanding where we are in the cycle can give you some context for some of the market movements. On average, most market corrections last about four months, but this can obviously vary widely depending on underlying causes and economic conditions.

It's also crucial to understand that corrections are not the same as crashes. While both of them involve some market decline, crashes are more severe, they're very sudden, and they're often triggered by specific events. The stock market crash of 1929, the 1987 crash, and the most recent COVID-19 crash in March 2020, are examples of some type of market crash rather than a correction.

I tell clients that the market's trend is upwards when you look at it over a 30-, 40-, or 50-year period. We have temporary downs and permanent ups. The S&P has averaged about 10% growth over a long period of time, but not without some really good years and some not so good years. The market rarely hits that exact number. There can be years when the market is up 28% or down 12%. The key is to keep your expectations in check and not expect a smooth ride of 10% every year. That is the average, not the norm.

The key during market declines or market corrections is to keep a long-term perspective. I know that can be hard when you're in the midst of bad news or the business channels reporting on declines daily or using words like "soar" or "plunge" every single time they report on the markets. Just know that corrections are a normal and healthy part of market cycles. Sometimes, the market needs to readjust valuations when they become too heated or over-inflated. Corrections can happen in any market, whether it's stocks, bonds, real estate, commodities, or even cryptocurrency. They can be broad, affecting an entire index like the S&P 500, or narrow, just impacting specific sectors or individual stocks. The key is staying the course and keeping a long-term perspective. Take your home, for example. It's one of your most important assets. Most people consider it a long-term investment. But if your home was in the paper and listed on the exchange on a business channel, and you saw the price of your home down 20% or 30%, you wouldn't panic and sell it because you know it's a long-term investment. That's the same way you need to look at your long-term investments for financial freedom or retirement.

To navigate a market decline or correction, it's important to stay calm and adhere to your plan and investment strategy. Here are some principles to live by:

1. **Don't panic and sell.** Emotional decisions often lead to really poor outcomes. If you panic, it is usually when fear is the highest and you will always find a reason to not get back in.
2. **Take this time to reassess your portfolio.** Review your holdings to ensure they align with your investment goals and risk tolerance. Maybe because tech stocks have done so well, you're now over-weighted in technology, which poses a risk to your portfolio if the market continues to decline.
3. **Look for buying opportunities.** Corrections can create chances to buy quality stocks or ETFs at discounted prices. Keep a watch list of stocks that you want to own but maybe didn't want to buy because they were near their 52-week high.
4. **Use this as an opportunity to harvest tax losses.** If some of your investments are in taxable accounts, you might be able to sell some losing positions to offset capital gains, potentially reducing your tax bill.

5. **Consider increasing your contributions.** A correction can be a good time to increase your retirement contributions. Even though a correction can be over before we know it, when markets decline for an extended period, I usually try to up my 401k contribution percentage. This allows me to buy at lower prices with a larger sum amount of money.

6. **Rebalance your portfolio.** During a correction, you might want to use it as an opportunity to rebalance your portfolio. If a correction has thrown your asset allocation out of whack, it can be a good time to add more in an area of your portfolio that is down.

7. **Stay informed, but avoid the noise.** The talking heads are going to be all over the business channels using those famous words: soar and plunge. Plunge is the most overused word in the business world when it comes to investments. Keep up with the market news, but be wary of some of these headlines that might fuel more panic.

8. **Maintain perspective.** Corrections are normal, and they're typically short-lived compared to the long-term market gains.

9. **Consider some defensive sectors.** If you're particularly concerned about the economy or the markets, you might want to shift some of your assets to defensive sectors like utilities, consumer staples, healthcare, or defense-related stocks.

You Don't Lose Unless You Sell

I can still remember when Warren Buffett was interviewed by CNBC during the 2008–2009 financial crisis. They asked him how much money he had lost. His answer was simple: "I didn't lose a dime because I didn't sell." So be like Warren Buffett. Don't panic and sell during market declines.

Now, we don't all have a mountain of cash sitting on the sidelines like Warren Buffett does to take advantage of opportunities in market declines. However, we can learn from Warren Buffett's advice. You don't lose unless you sell. So stay invested, stay calm, and stick with your plan, and you'll navigate all the future market declines that you'll face throughout your financial journey.

I've been a financial advisor for about 25 years. I started in the business in 1997. I remember how good it felt when everything that you recommended to your clients went up in value. During the peak of tech stocks, all the way until March 2000, you felt really confident about the future until you didn't. When everything crashed in March 2000, many tech stocks went down 60, 70, 80%, even the highest-quality tech stocks during that period, and it dragged the whole market down with them. The S&P 500 didn't go down as much as some of those tech stocks, of which many were part of the Nasdaq Index, and eventually rebounded from the lows to end the year down only 9.10%. If you panicked and sold, you would have missed out on some of that recovery. But the decline wasn't over; the S&P 500 was down 11.89% in 2001, and just when you thought things might get better, 2002 rolled around, and it was the worst year out of those three, sending the S&P 500 down another 22.10%.

Markets can do this and we sometimes forget that. The year 2000 was an exception. It was an extreme time of exuberance. Stocks with no earnings were flying high, and many investors were overweighted in tech stocks or using margin to enhance their returns. We sometimes forget that markets can go sideways or down for an extended period. That's always the fear when we have a correction. Anyone who has been investing long enough remembers that period from 2000 to 2002. They also remember the financial crisis and the Great Recession of 2008–2009, and the COVID-19 crash.

We always think that when we have a market correction, it's going to get worse, and that sometimes creates more fear and panic. Markets tend to go down more than people think they will. They also tend to go up further than anyone thinks. In the short term, markets are driven by fear and greed. In the long term, the markets are driven by a solid economy and growth in corporate earnings. The key is to be diversified in different industries, not to chase performance, and have the right mix of investments for your stage of life and risk tolerance. We can't predict the next extended downturn, we can only prepare ourselves that they will happen again during our investing journey.

When markets do go down, our minds go to that period when things kept going down. Markets tend to rebound quickly when we have these small corrections or inter-year declines if the economy is solid. If you get out of the market, you will always find a reason not to get back in. Stay invested. Time in the market is more important than timing.

> **Wise Wealth Tip**: When the markets are falling and the talking heads are saying the sky is falling, turn them off and go enjoy your life. This too will pass.

WEALTH DECISION #9: USE PASSIVE INVESTMENT STRATEGIES

Passive investing has gained tremendous popularity in recent years.

When I first got into the business in the late 1990s, actively traded mutual funds were the predominant way to invest. But today, ETFs make up a much larger part of the market. Most ETFs are passive investment strategies. It's an approach that can offer simplicity, lower costs, and potentially better long-term returns compared to active investing strategies.

But what exactly is passive investing, and how can you incorporate it into your financial plan?

Let's start with the basics. Passive investing is an investment strategy that aims to match the performance of a specific market index by keeping buying and selling to a minimum. This is in contrast to active investing, where fund managers actively buy and sell securities in an attempt to out-perform the market.

The most common form of passive investing is through index funds or ETFs. These track the market indexes, whatever particular index you're trying to match, whether that's small cap or mid cap or just trying to mir-ror the S&P 500. These funds or ETFs aim to replicate the performance of that target index by holding the same securities in the same proportions. There are also ETFs that attempt to buy the best of an index using specific criteria for identifying stocks with better profitability metrics. Companies like Avantus, WisdomTree, and Ark Investments are examples of invest-ment management companies that offer ETFs to attempt to buy the best of different areas of the market.

When it comes to index funds or ETFs that just try to match the market, you might be wondering why I would want to match the market instead of trying to beat it. It's an age-old question, and there are several compelling reasons to consider passive investing.

Number one, passive investing strategies have much lower costs. The expense ratios are much, much lower than actively managed funds because they require less research and fewer trades. The lower costs associated with passive investment strategies can have a significant impact on your long-term returns. Even a difference of 0.5% in annual fees can add tens of thousands of dollars over decades of investing.

Number two, they have consistent performance. When you look at an active mutual fund that tries to outperform in some years, studies have shown that the majority of active funds tend to underperform their benchmark indexes over the long term. So when you buy an index, you know what you're going to get. You're going to match that index, you're going to get broad diversification, and you're going to get simplicity.

Number three, passive investing can be just a much simpler way to implement a portfolio strategy compared to active strategies. You also get a ton of tax efficiency. With less buying and selling, passive funds tend to generate fewer taxable events. So, passive ETFs are a much better investment to hold, for instance, in a taxable investment account.

Number four, passive investing can help investors avoid the common behavioral mistake of chasing performance. Often an investor will look at a really good actively traded mutual fund and because it did really, really well in the last three or five years, they choose that fund, assuming that the performance of that particular fund will continue into the future.

Using Passive Investment Strategies

Here are some things to consider when using passive investment strategies:

1. **Educate yourself.**
   Read some online blogs about ETF investing. Learn about all the different index funds and ETFs available in the market – there are thousands to choose from. Understand their expense ratios, tracking errors, and the particular indexes they follow.
2. **Start small.**
   If you're new to passive investing, you don't need to overhaul your entire portfolio at once. You can start by allocating a portion of your investments to a broad market index fund and then start building it out from there. Analyze the mutual funds you have and compare those to ETFs in that same category. If the performance doesn't stack up and you're paying triple the fees, consider a low-cost ETF to replace that mutual fund in that particular category.

3. **Consider the different types of accounts you have and what strategies you use in them.**

   With your 401k, you're usually limited to the options in your plan. Typically, many of those are passive investment strategies or low-cost index funds.

   In your IRA or Roth IRA, you could use a combination of some active mutual funds in certain categories and the rest in passive investment strategies to cover those areas of the market for broad diversification.

   But if you have money in a taxable investment account, passive investment strategies are the most beneficial because they're not actively managed. There's no buying and selling going on throughout the year typically, so they are very tax efficient, and you won't get those big capital gains if the markets do well in a particular year.

   Passive investing is not an all-or-nothing approach. You can incorporate passive strategies into your portfolio and use them alongside some active strategies. Passive doesn't mean inactive. While the investments themselves are passively managed, you must actively manage your overall financial plan, including your asset allocation and risk management.

4. **Determine your asset allocation.**

   Before you start investing, it's critical to determine the right mix of stocks, bonds, and other assets based on your financial goals, your risk tolerance, and your time horizon. This is the one area where active decision-making is still important, even in a passive strategy.

5. **Choose the index funds or ETFs you'll use.**

   Look for funds that track broad market indexes with low expense ratios.

   Some popular options include total stock market index funds, S&P 500 index funds, the Russell 2000 index, the QQQ (Nasdaq), total international stock index mutual funds, and total bond market index funds.

6. **Implement a plan.**

Once you've chosen the funds or ETFs that are passive strategies, invest according to your predetermined asset allocation.

There are three different ways that you can use passive investment strategies in your portfolio.

You can buy index mutual funds, which track a specific market index. These funds offer simplicity and often have low minimum investment requirements, making them more accessible to most investors.

Number two is to invest in ETFs. ETFs are similar to index mutual funds, but they trade like stocks in exchange. They often have lower expenses than index mutual funds and offer more trading flexibility.

Third, you could buy a target-date fund. These funds automatically adjust the asset allocation as you approach a target date, which is usually retirement. While they're not purely passive, many of these use index funds as their underlying investments.

7. **Monitor your portfolio and rebalance it on a periodic basis.**

Even with a passive strategy, you'll need to rebalance your portfolio occasionally to maintain that target asset allocation. This might be done annually or when your allocation drifts 2%, 3%, or 5% from a threshold that you determine. For example, if you started with a mix of 70/30 stocks and bonds and the stock market does well enough in a particular year to push that allocation to 75/25, rebalance back to your original 70/30 mix.

8. **Stay the course.**

One of the biggest advantages of passive investing is simplicity, but it also requires discipline. You might be urged to react to short-term market movements or switch to active strategies based on the recent performance of a particular part of your portfolio. If you create an investment strategy based upon your financial goals, stick to it over the long term.

Do it on Your Own or Use a Robo-Advisor

You can certainly invest in passive investment strategies without the help of an advisor if that is how you want to spend your time or you feel comfortable managing things on your own.

If you don't use a financial advisor, there's always the option of using a robo-advisor. There are digital platforms out there that use algorithms to create and manage passive portfolios. You won't have a relationship with an individual advisor who can guide you and help you make important decisions, but this can be a good option if you want a hands-off approach and a simple portfolio tailored to your risk tolerance. The downfall of robo-advisors is they don't know you personally; they don't know your goals; they don't know your dreams; they don't know what your financial plan entails. But if you're looking for a simple way to invest, this could be a good option.

Common Questions and Maybe Misconceptions About Passive Investing

I'm often asked whether passive investing isn't just settling for average returns. I think while it's true that most passive investing aims to match market returns rather than beat them, it's important to remember that the average active fund manager underperforms the market after fees.

By aiming for market returns with lower costs, you may actually end up ahead of many active investors.

Another question I get is whether or not you need active management to protect you in a down market. It's a common belief that active managers can protect you during market downturns, but historical data doesn't really support this. In fact, many active managers struggle to time the market effectively. Some of those active money managers' funds are just way too big to make quick decisions to get in and out of the market. Because of the size of their fund, they can potentially move the market, and it can take months to get out of their positions.

Another question that comes up occasionally is whether you can combine passive and active strategies. I truly believe there are areas of the market where active money management can add value to your portfolio. Areas like value investing, emerging markets, some parts of the fixed income market, and small cap tend to be areas where active management can add some value and are worth considering for the active part of your investment portfolio.

Some investors use a core-satellite approach, where they take the core of their portfolio – maybe 70% to 80% in broad-based passive ETFs and index mutual funds – and seek additional returns with sector funds, emerging markets, individual stocks, or other things that can potentially add returns on top of the index-type returns.

Remember that the most important aspect of any investment strategy is that it aligns with your personal financial goals, risk tolerance, and time horizon.

Wise Wealth Tip: Buy five low-cost ETFs that cover large cap, mid cap, small cap, emerging markets, and international developed markets to start your investment journey. A simple growth asset allocation might be 40% in large cap, 20% in mid cap, 10% in small cap, 20% in international developed markets, and 10% in emerging markets. If you are close to retirement, consider adding some fixed income funds or ETFs. The asset allocation you choose should be based upon your age, goals, and risk tolerance.

WEALTH DECISION #10: CREATE A FINANCIAL PLAN

I believe a financial plan can increase your overall well-being and make you feel good that you have a plan in place and are headed in the right direction. When it comes to your financial goals, a comprehensive financial plan should include a detailed analysis of your income, expenses, an assessment of your current investments and retirement savings, and your debts. One of the most important elements of a financial plan is establishing a true budget, knowing what you need to meet your needs, wants, and wishes. A budget will help you identify areas where you can reduce spending and increase savings.

A financial plan will help you determine whether you are on track to meet your long-term financial goals and achieve all the things that are important to you. It will be yours and yours alone and should be updated each year as things change.

A solid financial plan should also be stress tested against different potential situations, like market volatility, potential tax increases, longevity, unexpected medical expenses like long-term care, and potential higher inflation. Most financial planning software used by financial advisors will assign a probability score that shows what the probability of success will be using Monte Carlo analysis, which runs your financial plan through a thousand different scenarios, good, bad, and ugly, and assigns a probability of success percentage. A solid plan should have between 75% and 90% probability of success. This is known as the confidence zone and will give you the best chance to make sure your money lasts through a long retirement. If you are below 75%, you can run different what-if scenarios and show in real time how to get your plan in the confidence zone. It can show you what would happen if you saved more, reduced your expenses, postponed retirement by one to four years, or got a part-time job for the first two to three years of retirement.

A financial plan can also show you how to maximize Social Security benefits and include strategies for protecting your assets and managing risk. This may include insurance policies, emergency savings, and estate planning.

Having a financial plan can provide you with a sense of control over your finances and reduce financial stress. It enables you to make informed decisions about your money, leading to better financial outcomes.

At Momentous Wealth Advisors, we follow a process called the Momentous W.E.A.L.T.H. Process for developing a financial plan for our clients. We start by discussing your ideal life, goals, and desires. We then build a financial plan and investment strategy centered around helping you achieve your most important financial goals.

The Momentous **W.E.A.L.T.H.** Process:

W – WHAT IS MOST IMPORTANT TO YOU?

What are your retirement needs, wants, and wishes? What are your expectations? What are your biggest concerns?

- Do you want to leave a legacy when you are gone?
- Do you want to travel in retirement?
- Do you want to be debt-free?
- Do you want to help your kids or grandkids with college?
- Do you want to move to a warmer climate?
- Are there certain charities you are passionate about?
- What do you want your money to accomplish?

E – EXPENSES AND INCOME SOURCES

- What are your expenses now to live a comfortable life?
- What income sources will you have at retirement?
- Should you take Social Security early or postpone it, to maximize your benefit for you and your spouse?
- Will you work part-time during part of your retirement?
- What major expenses do you anticipate in the short term?
- Do you want to have a vacation property in a warmer destination?

A – ASSETS AND LIABILITIES

What is your complete financial situation? What do you have in savings or emergency accounts? What do you owe on your mortgage or second property? How much do you have saved in your work retirement plans? What do you have in credit card debt? Do you have a goal to pay off debts by retirement?

We help analyze:

- Your current investment mix.
- Your risk tolerance and matching that with the right mix to reach your goals.
- Concentrated positions in stocks.
- Fees, expenses, and performance.

L – LONGEVITY RISK

Is there a history of longevity in your family? We don't know our end date, but this can be factored into your financial plan to make sure your money lasts longer than you do.

We will assess:

- How soon can you retire?
- What would happen if you lived longer than your life expectancy?
- Is your estate plan in order?

T – TAXES

Taxes play a major part in a client's retirement. What types of accounts you have and where you take money from first will be discussed to optimize your after-tax income. Do you typically get a refund or pay in? We have a service that allows us to analyze your tax return to find planning opportunities to reduce taxes now or in the future.

During our working years, most look for ways to reduce income. For clients retiring, we need to focus on how we can create a tax-efficient plan for income.

We will look at:

- Your Federal and State income tax rates.
- Dividend, interest, and capital gains taxes.
- Potential estate taxes at the end of your plan.
- Retirement distributions.
- Social Security taxation.

Wealth Strategies:

- Asset types: IRA, Roth IRAs, and Taxable Accounts.
- Sequence of distribution.
- Roth conversions if beneficial.
- Qualified dividend income in taxable accounts.
- Tax-loss harvesting strategies.

H – HEALTHCARE AND INSURANCE

Will your company healthcare cover insurance if you retire early? If not, we factor health insurance costs into your financial plan on top of your needs, wants, and wishes. We also look at protecting your plan against unexpected medical expenses like long-term care. We can stress-test for long-term care costs as they can be a significant risk to a financial plan. If you have ever had to care for an aging parent, you know all too well the costs associated with long-term care today.

If you don't know where to start when creating a financial plan, consider hiring a fiduciary financial advisor who focuses on financial planning.

Hiring a Fee-Based Fiduciary Advisor Who Focuses on Financial Planning

A financial advisor who is a fee-only fiduciary has a legal obligation to put your interests first. They have no proprietary products to sell and do not make commissions. Having a fiduciary financial advisor who puts your interests first and helps you build a financial plan will be crucial to helping you reach your long-term financial goals, whether that is financial security, financial independence, or financial freedom.

They are there to be your behavioral coach, to help you create the right investment mix for your risk tolerance and stage of life, to ensure you stay on track to retire on your terms, and to help you make important wealth decisions along your financial journey.

Here are the top six questions to ask a financial advisor.

1. Are you a Fiduciary 100% of the Time?

A fiduciary financial advisor is obligated to put your interests first. A fiduciary is also prohibited from selling you a financial product for a commission. Their compensation must come directly in the form of fees from you and be transparent. A fiduciary should have no conflicts of interest that prevent them from offering prudent tailored investment advice.

2. What is my Total "all-in" Cost to Work With you?

Just because a financial advisor is a fiduciary, does not mean it's easy to understand the all-in costs. Here are some of the common fees you might pay when working with a fiduciary financial advisor:

- Advice Fees. These can be one-time financial planning fees or a percentage of your investments.
- Transaction Fees. These are charged by the custodian (e.g., Schwab) when your advisor buys or sells investments on your behalf.
- Expense Ratios. A mutual fund or exchange-traded fund charges this fee to cover operational expenses.

3. What Experience do You Have With Financial Planning?

A financial advisor's experience is not just the years they have been in business. What is their experience with:

- Reducing taxes in retirement.
- Creating tax-efficient income in retirement.
- Lowering risk while maximizing investment returns.
- Increasing tax deductions through charitable giving.
- What certifications do you have?

4. Will you Provide me With a Comprehensive List of Your Advisory Services?

Asking a financial advisor for a list of their services will help you understand if they:

1. Have documented processes and procedures in place to care for their clients.
2. Focus on one particular area of wealth management or if they take a holistic approach.
3. Charge extra for creating a financial plan. Is that a one-time fee or ongoing?

Some advisors might offer more add-on services such as stock option optimization, Roth IRA conversion analysis, Social Security planning, and charitable giving.

5. Where do you Keep my Money?

Does your financial advisor use a reputable third-party custodian to hold your investment/retirement accounts? Some well-known custodians include Fidelity, Schwab, and Pershing.

6. What is Your Investment Philosophy?

Ask them about their investment philosophy and approach to managing your money.

Does the advisor use low-cost index funds? Do they actively trade individual stocks? Additional investment questions to consider asking a financial advisor include:

- How do you advise on investments held in a retirement plan at work like a 401(k) or 403(b)?
- How many positions do you include in most clients' investment portfolios?

- Can you incorporate individual stock positions that I don't want to sell?
- Do you have a process for tax-loss harvesting?
- What is your process for screening investments like mutual funds, ETFs, or stocks?

Hiring a financial advisor can be crucial to helping you work toward building more wealth for yourself and your family. This is especially important as you reach your 50s and want to retire on your terms and stay comfortably retired.

Wise Wealth Tip: Interview two or three financial advisors and make your decision based upon their experience and if they found out what was important to you, but more importantly, how they made you feel.

Summary of Wealth Decisions to Live a Richer Life

Making better financial decisions requires knowledge and a wealth-building mindset. If you are not where you want to be, the time to start is now.

If you feel good about where you are and have been saving and investing for years but want a plan to achieve financial freedom, go to Chapter 6, where I discuss a 9-Step Plan to Achieve Financial Freedom in depth.

If you are very close to retirement or just retired, skip to Chapter 7, where I discuss the 9-Step Plan to Retire and Stay Comfortably Retired.

If you are starting with investing for your future, here are some small ways to incorporate wealth principles into your life and become smarter with money over your first year:

First 90-Day Period:

1. Look at your budget and find out where you can cut things out so you can live below your means.
2. Invest in your 401k if eligible, at least 5% of your income or enough to get the full match from your employer.
3. Set up an emergency fund and put at least $200/month in a high-interest money market account.

Second 90-Day Period:

1. Make a plan to pay off high-interest debt.
2. Increase your monthly contribution from 5% to 7% to your 401k.
3. Start a Roth IRA and start investing a minimum of $100 per month.

Third 90-Day Period:

1. Listen to the Wealth Decisions by Brian Podcast to educate yourself on wealth and mindset principles.
2. Increase your monthly contribution from 7% to 10% to your 401k.
3. Develop a simple financial plan.

Fourth 90-Day Period:

1. Increase your contributions to your Roth IRA by $100–200 per month.
2. Start a HSA if you have the option at your work.
3. Invest your Roth IRA more aggressively than your 401k to maximize tax-free growth.

One year from now, you will have made progress on building your wealth by paying yourself first, which will become your new standard. You will feel better about your finances, have a plan for your money, and be on a path toward living a richer life.

MOMENTOUS DECLARATION #8

Instead of thinking about how much money I don't have, I will think about how much money I will have in the future with my plan for financial independence or freedom.

CHAPTER SIX

THE WEALTH DECISIONS PLAN TO ACHIEVE FINANCIAL FREEDOM

A Wealth Decisions Plan gives you a plan with actions in order of importance to achieve financial freedom. This is designed for anyone 10–25 years away from retirement. There are many crucial wealth decisions I think you need to make along your financial journey. But one thing we haven't discussed is the order of importance in terms of those decisions that you need to make along this path toward retirement, financial independence, or financial freedom. So here is a 9-Step Plan to Achieve Financial Freedom.

Step 1:   Save your first three months of expenses in an emergency account.

The goal is to have at least six months in an emergency account eventually, but the first step is to save at least three months. Determine what you need each month to cover your basic needs. Take that number and multiply it by three. Set up a money market account to automatically save a percentage of your income until you have at least three months' worth. Keep that money market away from your checking and savings accounts. Keep it in another bank account or an investment account at a brokerage firm. While you're doing that, continue to contribute to your 401k, but contribute what you need to contribute to get your match.

Step 2:   Get rid of high-interest debt.

Whether you have one credit card or multiple credit cards, you have to get out of debt. Debt is a wealth killer. Focus on your smallest credit card first – the one on which you owe the least – and get rid of that. I think the debt snowball is very effective: which is the Dave Ramsey approach. The debt snowball method is a strategy for paying off credit card debt that involves paying your smallest balances first and paying the minimum on all other cards. Once the smallest debt is paid off, apply the extra money toward the next smallest debt. You then keep repeating this process until all debts are paid off. Have a goal of when you want to have all your cards paid off. Take your credit card out of your wallet, put it in your freezer, in your sock drawer, or cut it up.

Step 3:   Contribute a minimum of 10% in your Roth 401k option unless you're in the highest tax bracket.

Many individuals invest primarily in the pre-tax option of their 401k. Depending on your tax bracket, contributing to the Roth option in your 401k will help you create a more tax-efficient income when you retire.

If you are in a lower tax bracket, consider investing mostly in the Roth 401k option. If you are in the mid tax bracket, split it equally between pre-tax and Roth. If you are in the highest tax bracket, split it 70/30 between pre-tax and Roth 401k contributions. Consider consulting a financial advisor to determine the best mix for your situation.

If you're in the highest tax bracket possible, combine pre-tax and Roth 401k contributions. And if you have a job where you get a year-end bonus, up your pre-tax contribution to 20% to 40% just for the bonus period to avoid those high taxes that bonuses tend to get.

Step 4: Contribute the maximum you possibly can to a Health Savings Account.

The maximum in 2024 was $4,150 for individuals and $8,300 for families. Invest your contributions in a mix appropriate for your stage in life and risk tolerance.

I typically see people have HSAs that are all invested in a stable value fund. They forget to look at investing that because we don't think of health savings accounts the same as we do 401ks. But make sure you invest that money inside the HSA. HSAs are a great tool because it's pre-tax money going in there. They're basically triple tax-exempt. And then, if you use that money for expenses down the road that are related to medical expenses or deductibles, it comes out tax-free. So they're a great tool to have as another account that you can draw from in retirement for specific things related to health care.

Step 5: Add three more months of expenses in your emergency account.

Go back to your emergency account and focus on adding an additional three months to your emergency money market account. Keep it in a separate account, again, not in the same place as your checking or savings. If an emergency comes up and you take money out of that account, try to replenish it back to six months of expenses to be covered in case of future emergencies.

Step 6:   Max out your retirement plan.

If 10% is insufficient to max out your plan at work, contribute what you need to max out your work retirement plan. For example, the maximum in 2025 is $23,500. If you're over 50, you can contribute $7,500 with a catch-up provision in 2025, but this amount is subject to change in the future. Check the current maximums by doing a Google search of 401k contribution limits in the current year.

Step 7:   Max your Roth IRA, convert your IRA to a Roth, or use the Backdoor Roth strategy.

Maxing out a Roth IRA is crucial because all the money you put into a Roth IRA grows tax-free, and your retirement income comes out tax-free. The contribution limits have steadily risen over the years, giving individuals opportunities to put away more money for retirement. For example, in the year 2025, you could contribute $7,000 to a Roth IRA. Also, if you were over the age of 50 in 2025, you could make a catch-up contribution of $1,000, which would allow you to put a total of $8,000 into a Roth IRA. Look up the current contribution limits and catch-up provisions by doing a Google search.

One thing to be aware of is that the government has imposed income limits on whether you can contribute to a Roth IRA. You can look up the current income contribution limits to see if you are eligible.

If you have an existing IRA, think about partially converting some of your IRA to a Roth IRA by looking at how much room is in your current tax bracket. For example, if your income is $170,000 and there is $30,000 left before you get bumped up to the next tax bracket, you could safely convert anything under $30,000 and still stay in the same tax bracket. If you use this strategy each year, you must reevaluate your income tax bracket if you convert money in any given year. Consult a financial advisor before you think about converting a traditional IRA to a Roth IRA.

If you don't have an existing IRA and are not eligible to contribute to a Roth IRA because your income is too high, you can use the Backdoor Roth Strategy to contribute to a Roth IRA. To do that, you contribute to a nondeductible IRA, then immediately convert it to a Roth IRA. That's called the Backdoor Roth IRA. So, if you're over the income limits, there are still ways to get money invested in a Roth IRA. If you have an existing IRA, consult a financial advisor, as there can be tax consequences to using this strategy.

Step 8:   Invest in taxable and after-tax accounts.

Many of us focus mostly on our 401ks for saving for retirement, but a taxable investment account is also an important tool, especially if you want to retire early (before age 59½). If you have additional money you can save, start dollar cost averaging money into a taxable investment account for the long term. Taxable investment accounts have preferential tax treatment with long-term capital gains; just be aware that any investment held less than a year is taxed at your current tax rate. Long-term capital gains are taxed at 0%, 15%, or 20% depending on your income level. Another option for super funding your retirement is taking advantage of the after-tax option in your 401k. This is sometimes referred to as the Mega-Roth Strategy.

After-Tax Option: The Mega-Roth Strategy

I know I have been talking about all these different Backdoor Roth Strategies and Conversion Strategies, but the Mega-Roth is a way to superfund your retirement. So, ask your employer if there's an after-tax option in your 401k.

If you don't have this after-tax option, I suggest investing in a taxable investment account as much as possible on top of the other contributions you're making for retirement. One thing to note is that your employer plan must have an in-service withdrawal option. So you'll be able to contribute to this after-tax option and then roll it into your Roth IRA at the end of the year.

You want to ensure that your total contributions to your pre-tax 401k, your Roth 401k, and your employer contributions and this after-tax option do not exceed the 415 limit. Be sure to check every year what the limit is as they can change from year to year.

For example, if you invested the max in your 401k in 2024 along with a catch-up provision because you're over 50, you could contribute $30,500 yourself with that catch-up provision. If your company makes matching contributions of $12,500, you take those two numbers and add them up: ($30,500 + $12,500 = $43,000). Then, subtract that number from the 415 limit in 2024, which was $69,000. This will tell you how much you could contribute to an after-tax option in your 401k in that year on top of your 401k personal and matching contributions. In this example you could contribute $26,000 into an after-tax option in your plan ($69,000 – $43,000 = $26,000).

Step 9:   Pay down your mortgage.

Figure out what you need to pay monthly to pay down your mortgage by the time you retire. Consider refinancing potentially to a 15-year mortgage. Also, think about adopting a bi-weekly payment toward your mortgage. That will help pay it down even quicker.

If you would like to see a sample 9-Step Wealth Decisions Plan to Achieve Financial Freedom, go to: https://www.momentouswealthadvisors.com/wealthdecisionsplan.

CHAPTER SEVEN

THE RETIREMENT DECISIONS PLAN TO RETIRE AND STAY COMFORTABLY RETIRED

For those who are about to retire or who have just retired, this chapter will discuss the 9-Step Retirement Decisions Plan to Retire and Stay Comfortably Retired. Even if you are years away from retirement, this chapter will give you valuable information on things to think about as you approach retirement.

It's a plan in order of importance to make sure that you do the right things to ensure that your money lasts long into retirement and works for all your most important financial goals.

Step 1:   Save at least 12 months of expenses for short- and mid-term goals.

Determine what you need each month to cover your basic needs, and then take that number and multiply it by 12. Part of this emergency account could be invested, not just in a high-yield money market account. You could potentially put half of this account in short-term CDs, and short- to intermediate-term fixed income ETFs.

This is different than the suggestion for the amount recommended when you are working, because when you are retired and taking money from your investments to live, you want to have a larger safety net available if we have extended periods of market underperformance. Because you don't have an income from a job anymore, having more money liquid will give you more flexibility and peace of mind knowing you have something to draw from for travel, short- or mid-term goals, helping the kids or grandkids with college, or other expenses that come up in retirement.

Step 2:   Get rid of high-interest debt.

If you have high-interest credit cards, you need to get that debt paid off when you retire. Use that credit card for travel expenses, but only if you can pay off that amount very quickly.

Step 3:   Determine your true budget for retirement.

You're going to want to factor in your wants and wishes on top of your basic needs, and that would include travel, charitable giving, or helping the kids or grandkids with college. You will also want to factor in your healthcare costs if you're retiring before the age of Medicare eligibility, which is 65.

Figuring out your true budget is essential to make sure that your retirement works for you. Running all the different types of budgets you could have through a financial plan is important to make sure that you understand what wiggle room you have in retirement.

Have a financial advisor run different budget scenarios to show you how well your plan will hold up long-term.

Step 4:   Determine your asset allocation.

You can't afford to make mistakes when you retire. You want the right mix of investments to create a sustainable income. You typically can't invest your money the same way you did before retirement. Investing in retirement is a very different animal. You need to have a balanced approach with less volatility and fewer ups and downs to allow you to take an income for retirement from your portfolio. This means having some bonds, fixed income funds, or ETFs, in addition to a well-thought-out mix of dividend-producing stocks, low-cost index mutual funds, and ETFs in all the asset classes that make up a diversified portfolio. The proper allocation for you depends on your risk tolerance, income needs, and financial goals.

If you don't need to take money from your portfolio, which is a nice problem to have, and maybe you have a really high Social Security benefit and a really nice pension, you can invest that portfolio a little differently.

If your goal is to leave a legacy and you don't need as much from your portfolio to live during retirement, you could invest that money in more growth-oriented investments.

Asset allocation is crucial when you retire. Having the right mix is super important to make sure that money continues to work for you long-term and keeps up with inflation, but it also lowers the volatility of your portfolio so that you can take an income more effectively.

Step 5:   Develop your income withdrawal strategy.

I suggest taking no more than 5% out of your retirement accounts per year, and you can set that up as a monthly withdrawal so it feels just like a paycheck. You will likely want to take this 5% from pre-tax accounts first, taxable accounts second, and Roth IRA accounts third, but where you take money from first depends on your particular situation.

Have a financial advisor create a financial plan and run what-if scenarios with different returns and withdrawal rates to ensure your plan works long-term.

If you have a pension or high Social Security benefit, you want to develop a withdrawal strategy that's maybe a different mix than normal. Maybe the majority is from a taxable account, maybe some is from a tax-deferred account, and some is from a Roth IRA. Look at your tax bracket to ensure you can continue to stay in that tax bracket and create the most tax-efficient income possible in retirement.

Step 6:   Optimize your Social Security benefits.

You may consider postponing your Social Security to maximize benefits for you and your spouse. Typically, you want to do this when there's one person who has a really high benefit and the other a low benefit. If the person with the higher benefit were to pass away, the surviving spouse would get the higher benefit as a survivor that would continue for their life. One thing to note is that the surviving spouse only gets one benefit. Theirs or yours, whichever is higher. That is why maximizing the higher benefit by delaying Social Security may be the wisest decision you can make. Have a financial advisor run a Social Security analysis to determine the optimal strategy for you to take to maximize your benefits and to make your plan work better in the long term.

Step 7:   Consider Roth conversion strategies.

Consider partially converting your IRA to a Roth IRA by looking at how much room is in your tax bracket. It's tough in retirement to suddenly convert your IRA to a Roth and have that resulting tax bill. You certainly need to be able to afford to pay the taxes now from a taxable investment account or savings.

The benefit would be that down the road, when you're 78, 80, 82, and those required minimum distributions (RMDs) on an IRA start to be a much higher amount percentage-wise, which could potentially bump you up to the next tax bracket. For example, if you are 84 years old and have 3 million in an IRA, your RMD will be around 6% based upon current

RMD Life Expectancy Factors. That means you are forced to take $180,000 out of your IRA whether you need the income or not.

So, think about converting some of those IRAs partially each year over a period of time while staying in the same tax bracket. Whatever room is in your tax bracket, say there's $20,000, you could safely convert $15,000 a year from your IRAs to Roth IRAs over a period of time to try to get more in Roth money to benefit you and your family in the future. Currently, leaving an IRA to your children today requires them to have to take all that money out within 10 years. For example, if you leave them $3 million in an IRA, they would have to take out at least $300k a year, which would most likely bump them up to the highest tax bracket. They cannot stretch your IRA out over their lifetime. But with Roth IRAs, you don't have to do that. There's no required minimum distribution and no taxes. Having more Roth IRA assets can be a great legacy planning tool.

Step 8:   Consider creating a personal pension plan.

A pension plan is basically an annuity product created by your company to give you options for lifetime income for you and your spouse. You can also create a personal pension plan, just like a pension someone would get from working at a company for many years. A pension is an insurance product that gives you a guaranteed income for your life and potentially for the life of your spouse if you choose the 100% survivor option. You can do that same thing today with low-cost indexed annuities with income riders or fee-based variable annuities with income riders that guarantee an income over your lifetime as well. It all depends on your particular situation.

When looking at annuities, be aware of your options and avoid high-cost variable annuities with high Mortality and Expense (M&E) ratios, and expensive riders.

A lot of times, when I meet with people and look at their income sources and their portfolio, I don't always suggest that they buy an annuity. Annuities are very expensive, especially those sold by insurance agents who make a commission. Annuities can be a great way to create some extra guaranteed income, but just be careful of all the high costs, long surrender schedules, and annuities sold by insurance companies with poor ratings.

Step 9:   Pay off your mortgage.

Figure out what you need to pay extra each month to get your mortgage paid off. Consider refinancing to a 15-year mortgage if feasible. Consider paying bi-monthly, if possible, to speed up that payment. I don't think it's necessary to have your mortgage paid off when you retire, but it all depends on your budget and what you need to live comfortably.

There's a huge peace of mind knowing that one of your most important assets is paid off.

So to retire and stay comfortably retired, a lot of crucial retirement decisions need to be made on an ongoing basis. One thing I didn't mention in this retirement decisions plan is unexpected medical expenses.

If there were a tenth step, it would be to evaluate the need for long-term care insurance. Usually, I do a stress test on a client's financial plan against an unexpected medical expense like long-term care. If the plan holds up, if there is potentially that type of need somewhere down the road in retirement, then we don't look at insuring their plan with a long-term care insurance policy.

But if we do a stress test and it definitely impacts their plan and brings them well below the confidence zone to make sure their money lasts, then we'll explore those options.

To see an example of the 9-Step Retirement Decisions Plan that outlines the nine steps needed to retire and stay comfortably retired, go to: https://www.momentouswealthadvisors.com/retirementdecisions.

CHAPTER EIGHT

HEALTH DECISIONS FOR A RICHER LIFE

It is essential to prioritize your health above everything else, including your wealth. Without good health, you cannot enjoy your life to the fullest, regardless of how financially stable you are. Taking care of your physical and mental well-being should be your priority, because it affects your overall quality of life. Make health your keystone habit. When health becomes your keystone habit, everything else falls into place easier. A keystone habit is the habit you put above everything. You protect it and make it a priority.

We all know, as we age, we may experience a range of health issues and chronic diseases such as diabetes, high blood pressure, heart disease, and arthritis, as well as mental health conditions such as depression and anxiety. But what if we didn't have as many of those things to worry a lot about? What if, instead of being reactive, we become proactive about our health? Easier said than done, but essential if we want to be active and healthy long into our retirement years.

The big question is, if we are not where we want to be with our health right now, why? We want to lose weight or get fitter, but every time we start, we don't keep going and end up right back where we started. The biggest reason we don't stick with a workout routine or diet is that we don't have enough reasons to keep us going. We don't have a why behind the why that keeps us inspired long-term. We will dig into finding out the why behind your why in the 7 Steps chapter.

To create a healthy life, some important decisions need to be made centered around our health and well-being. The following 10 health decisions are some of the most important decisions to make to set yourself up to live a healthy lifestyle. I am sure there are many more, but these are the 10 I think are the most beneficial to help you live a long-term healthy lifestyle, increase your energy, and live a richer life.

HEALTH DECISION #1: ADOPT A HEALTHY LIFESTYLE MINDSET

"Eat your food as medicines. Otherwise, you will eat your medicines as food."
– Best-awarded words in London

Having a healthy lifestyle mindset is a journey, not an overnight change. It starts with adding positive changes to your life that eventually become part of who you are. Every day your body keeps score, so eat healthy, think healthy, and be healthy. Adopting a healthy lifestyle mindset is crucial to becoming healthier over time. A healthy lifestyle is not about dieting. Dieting doesn't work in the long run because it deprives you of things. Working out is more about feeling good, not just looking good. A healthy lifestyle is not about being skinny enough to wear a size 2 if you are a woman, or a having a 32-inch waist if you are a man. It's about a commitment to be healthy from the inside out. It's about taking care of your body, so that as you age, you still have the energy to live a more vibrant life.

It has been said that at each moment of our lives, we either invoke or destroy our dreams. Whether we reach or don't reach a goal comes down to whether it is now a commitment in our mind or just a thought. When you are committed to doing something, you will do whatever it takes. When you're not, you will find yourself making the same old excuses. You first need to understand why you are where you are now before you can understand and know how you can get to where you deserve to be. Not living a healthy lifestyle is not a single cataclysmic event. You don't become unhealthy overnight. Poor health is simply a result of a few errors in judgment repeated every day. My goal is to help you stop that cycle. It first starts with your mindset.

When you shift your mindset from knowing something is possible to knowing it is possible for you, that is when things change. Losing weight requires an identity shift, which I discussed in Chapter 1. Maybe you have always struggled with your weight, and sometimes there are genetics at work that make it hard for you to be fit. Maybe you were super fit in high school, but you let yourself go, and you have accepted that, with age, that is just the way it is now. But you don't have to accept that new story you have created for yourself. You can change your mindset and your identity. As you keep introducing new things slowly into your life toward living a healthy lifestyle, you will start to feel like it is becoming part of who you are. You will feel like a health-conscious person and start to act that way more when you are faced with temptations. You will eventually crave healthy foods the same way you maybe crave fast or junk food now. You will become more disciplined with healthy choices because you will have a bigger reason to be healthy and it will become your new standard.

One of my favorite quotes by the godfather of self-development, Jim Rohn, is, "We must all suffer one of two things: the pain of discipline or the pain of regret. The pain of discipline weighs ounces, and the pain of regret weighs tons." If you don't adopt a healthy lifestyle, one day, the pain of regret will envelop your mind because you know you could have done something about it. It is much easier to adopt a healthy lifestyle mindset when you know what you want for your health, have a why behind your why, set new standards, and have a long-term vision with a short-term plan, which we will go into in depth in the 7 Steps chapter. I believe better health will give you more energy to focus more on all the other things in life that will create more meaning and allow you to enjoy all the experiences that life can offer. You won't have as many limitations on what you can do.

I heard an analogy from Brendon Burchard, a motivational author and speaker, who said, "The power plant doesn't have energy. It transforms and generates energy. We don't have happiness. We generate happiness." And it's the same with our health. We don't have good health; we generate good health. What are you doing to create energy, happiness, or good health? What's draining your energy? What's feeding it? Well food is one of the main sources of your energy – or lack thereof.

Certain foods give you energy, and certain ones take it away. You need to know what to eat if you are going to adopt a healthy lifestyle.

Foods That Drain Your Energy

It is very normal for our energy levels to rise and fall throughout each day. Our energy level has a lot to do with what we put in our body, which we have complete control over. Here are some foods that will drain your energy.

1. White bread, pasta, rice: they may have carbs but they are full of processed grains. They may give you some short-term energy, but processed grains give a quick rise in blood sugar and insulin levels, followed by a drop in energy.
2. Breakfast cereals: most breakfast cereals are loaded with added sugar. Sugars make up as much as 50% of the total carbs found in

most popular cereals. The combination of high sugar and low fiber content spikes your blood sugar and insulin, giving you a burst of energy and then a crash.

3. Coffee: I love coffee but try to consume it in moderation. It has been said that coffee doesn't actually give you energy or wake you up, it just tricks the receptors in your brain. Drinking too much caffeine will result in mid-afternoon crashes.

4. Energy drinks: They may give you a burst of energy, but many energy drinks have over 50 grams of sugar and 200 mg of caffeine, which is the equivalent of four cups of coffee.

5. Fried and fast food: These are high in fat and low in fiber, which will drain your energy. Eating food with high amounts of the wrong type of fats will make you feel full and sluggish.

Foods That Give You Energy

To have more energy throughout your day you need to focus on eating more nutrient-dense foods.

1. Complex carbohydrates found in things like rolled oats and sweet potatoes are great fuel sources, releasing glucose slowly to maintain steady energy levels. I have grown to love overnight oats and have a great sweet potato soup recipe I make at least once a week.

2. Iron-rich leafy greens like spinach and kale help oxygen flow efficiently through your bloodstream. That sweet potato soup recipe I make is my favorite way to eat kale, or if you haven't tried sautéing kale with olive oil and garlic, put that one on your list.

3. Protein found in things such as eggs, lentils, and almonds provides lasting stamina and helps repair muscle tissue. I eat egg whites and almonds daily.

4. Bananas have a perfect blend of natural sugars and fiber for quick and sustained energy.

5. Healthy fats found in things like avocados and chia seeds help keep your mental focus sharp and get you some Omega-3s. I try to eat an avocado (sprinkled with sea salt) every other day for breakfast.

6. Quinoa seed has a complete protein profile along with some essential B vitamins that help convert food into energy. Put some quinoa seeds in your morning smoothie or top your salad with them.

7. Matcha green tea powder has a combination of caffeine and L-theanine, which gives you a calm alertness without the jittery crash of coffee.

8. Deep-colored berries like blueberries and goji berries are packed with antioxidants that fight fatigue at the cellular level.

9. Dark chocolate is rich in theobromine and magnesium, which can help power you through afternoon slumps. Dark chocolate is how I get my sweet tooth fix.

Maintaining high energy levels is not just about what you eat, but in when you eat your meals throughout the day. Starting your morning with a combination of rolled oats topped with chia seeds and berries creates an awesome combo. The oats provide steady glucose release, while the chias' Omega-3s support brain function, and the berries' antioxidants kick-start your metabolism. If you get up early, the perfect pre-workout breakfast is a mashed banana on sprouted grain toast with some honey and cinnamon. The banana provides fast-acting fuel, the complex carbohydrates in sprouted grain offer sustained energy, and the cinnamon helps regulate blood sugar.

For mid-morning, try having an apple with almond butter, which balances blood sugar and helps provide some sustained energy.

For lunch, combine some quinoa or brown rice with legumes and dark leafy greens, along with some free-range chicken for extra protein.

For your mid-afternoon snack, during the notorious 3 p.m. slump, try having a small handful of almonds with a few dried apricots. These work together to fight fatigue and they are easy to have with you on the go.

When planning dinner, have some sweet potatoes with iron-rich foods like lentils or spinach. The sweet potato's vitamin C content increases iron absorption, setting you up for better energy levels the next day. Have some chicken, salmon, or lean meat to go along with dinner to get your lean protein.

What You Should Eat?

BEEF:

Grass-fed / Free-range or Free roaming / Raised without antibiotics/No antibiotics administered.

POULTRY:

Natural / Free-range / Free roaming / Fresh / Certified organic / Cage free / Certified humane raised and handled.

EGGS:

Cage free / Free-range / Hormone-free / Antibiotic-free / Organic / Vegetarian-fed / Omega-3 enriched / No added antibiotics / Pasture raised.

DAIRY:

Organic / No hormones (rBGH) / Antibiotic-free.

VEGETARIAN/VEGAN:

Almonds / Black beans / Chia seeds / Garbanzo beans (Chickpeas) / Greek yogurt / Hemp seed / Lentils / Peanut butter / Pumpkin seeds / Quinoa / Soybeans / Tofu.

FISH/SEAFOOD:

Salmon: Wild caught, Alaskan / Halibut, Atlantic / Catfish / Lobster / Oysters / Clams / Crab: King, Snow, and Tanner (AK) / Scallops (farmed), Shrimp/ Tilapia / Tuna: Albacore.

HIGH-QUALITY FATS:

Olives / Avocados / Almonds / Cashews / Macadamia nuts / Pine nuts / Brazil nuts / Pecans / Hazelnuts / Sunflower seeds / Pumpkin seeds / Chia seeds / Grass-fed butter / Olive oil (extra virgin) / Hemp oil / Hemp seeds / Avocado oil / Walnut oil / Walnuts / Flax oil.

A Healthy Lifestyle Is Not Just About Looking Good

In Tony Horton's book *The Big Picture*, he says, "There is nothing wrong with wanting to look your best, but what truly motivates and sustains you should go much, much deeper than muscle definition. It works a lot like that old gem 'money can't buy happiness.' You buy things that might make you happy for a day or two, but ultimately, you just end up buying more things to maintain that high. Similarly, when you make changes in your life for aesthetic reasons, you're never going to be content." Extreme diets to lose weight to look good are usually not sustainable. You end up not giving your body the calories it needs and your body ends up actually storing fat, because your body thinks it is starving and will hold onto fat to keep you alive. A healthy lifestyle is not about restricting calories, but giving your body what it needs. It is about feeling good, not just looking good.

Your Limitations Should Not Be Excuses

Your limitations may be challenges, but they should not be your excuses. There are so many things in life you can't control, but what you put in your mouth and what you do physically each day, you absolutely can change and have control over.

Maintaining a healthy lifestyle involves a positive mindset, regular physical activity, a balanced diet, and an overall commitment to well-being. See yourself as someone who could be healthy and fit again and start taking small actions focused on your health. Find a strong why for wanting to become healthier rather than just losing weight. Get an accountability partner or hang around other health-minded individuals, and you will be on your way to living a healthier life.

Top Three Books on Healthy Living

1. *The Big Picture* by Tony Horton.
2. *Outlive: The Science & Art of Longevity* by Peter Attia, MD.
3. *The Anti-Diet* by Christy Harrison.

In the 7 Steps chapter you will learn more about the M.A.D.E. LifePlan and will define what you want to accomplish with your health in the short and long term. You will create a 10-year vision and a plan to achieve what is most important to you when it comes to your health and well-being. Over 90 days, as part of your M.A.D.E. Life Action Plan, you will focus on One Momentous Thing you can do every day to start adopting a healthy lifestyle. Over time you will engrain healthy habits into your life and they will become part of who you are.

> **Wise Health Tip**: Make one commitment today to develop a healthy lifestyle mindset, like reading a book on healthy living, making your shopping list, joining a health-conscious community or gym with accountability coaches, or going for a walk after dinner.

HEALTH DECISION #2: INCORPORATE HIIT AND STRENGTH TRAINING INTO YOUR ACTIVE LIFESTYLE

High-intensity interval training (HIIT) may provide the same health benefits as regular exercise in less time by helping increase calorie burn, and reduce body fat, heart rate, and blood pressure. While most people know that working out is healthy, it's estimated that about 20% of people world-wide don't get enough of it each day; in the United States alone, that number is more like 80%. I get it; most of us feel that we don't have enough time to exercise (if this sounds like you, maybe it's time to try HIIT).

HIIT is a workout that involves short periods of intense exercise alternated with recovery periods. One of the biggest advantages of HIIT is that you can get more health benefits in minimal time. It is a super time-efficient way to exercise.

HIIT Benefits

1. HIIT can burn a lot of calories in a short amount of time. Researchers found that HIIT burned 25–30% more calories than the other forms of exercise.
2. Your metabolic rate is higher for hours after HIIT exercise. One of the ways HIIT helps is that you burn calories long after you're done exercising.
3. In addition to helping with fat loss, HIIT can help increase muscle mass because of the different strength exercises in a HIIT routine.
4. HIIT can improve oxygen consumption, which is your muscles' ability to use oxygen. It is like a form of endurance training.
5. HIIT can reduce your heart rate and blood pressure over time.
6. HIIT can also reduce blood sugar. A summary of 50 studies found that HIIT not only reduces blood sugar but also improves insulin resistance more than traditional continuous exercise.

During most HIIT workouts, you get some strength training, which becomes even more important as you age. In recent years, there has been a ton of new studies examining the benefits of strength training. These studies have revealed that strength training can positively impact not only physical fitness but also mental health and overall well-being. By incorporating some weight-lifting, resistance training, or bodyweight exercises into your fitness routine, you can improve bone density, increase muscle mass, and boost metabolism.

Strength training has also been shown to reduce the risk of chronic diseases such as heart disease, diabetes, and arthritis. When it comes to fat loss, strength training has some great benefits as well. First, strength training helps to increase lean muscle mass. This gives the body room to store fuel that would otherwise be turned into body fat. Second, it helps your body to burn more calories, even after the workout is over. This is because the more muscle mass you have, the more fuel your body needs to keep you going. This makes weight loss easier and more sustainable. Third, it helps your insulin system work better, which helps turn your store-fat signals down.

Be Active Each Day: NEAT (Non-exercise Activity Thermogenesis)

Another way to be active is through non-exercise activity. These are all of the activities we do outside of intentional exercise, like housework, grocery shopping, playing with your kids, standing at your desk instead of sitting, etc.

Example 7-Day Active Schedule:

Monday: HIIT Training.
Tuesday: Chest/Triceps/Biceps – a walk after dinner.
Wednesday: HIIT Training.
Thursday: Back/Shoulders/Legs – a walk after dinner.
Friday: Walk/Bike/Pickleball or Yoga.
Saturday: Chest/Triceps/Biceps – a mid-afternoon walk.
Sunday: Something Active Outside/Hike or Yoga.

Wise Health Tip: Put these activities in your phone as appointments with reminders. If you don't have a gym membership, you can find many great YouTube videos on 15-minute HIIT routines.

HEALTH DECISION #3: EAT A WHOLE FOODS DIET WITH PLENTY OF PROTEIN

A whole foods diet is about consuming foods that are as close to the natural state as possible. You typically find most of the whole foods on the outside aisles of the grocery store.

We have been told to eat our vegetables our whole lives, and for good reason. Eating dark leafy green vegetables, like kale, spinach, and collard greens, helps to provide your body with iron, magnesium, and B vitamins, all of which help to maintain proper energy levels. Iron helps to carry blood throughout the body and maintain oxygenation. I try to eat spinach at least three times a week and kale once or twice a week, but I have no interest in collard greens. If you like them, more power to you.

Having fruit in our diet is also essential. Some diets say to avoid eating too much fruit because of the sugar content. The difference is that unlike processed foods with added sugars, the sugar in fruit is natural, and fruit is packed with fiber and essential vitamins. The fiber in fruits also slows sugar absorption, preventing rapid blood sugar spikes that can happen when you eat refined sugars. Try to eat fruit with your breakfast or at least two meals per day. Blueberries, raspberries, blackberries, bananas, oranges, and any fruit you like. Use frozen fruit in your smoothies so you don't have to go to the grocery store so often. There are just too many benefits to having fruit in your diet not to have them as part of a balanced diet. You get better immune health, gut health, and a reduction in inflammation. Also, research consistently associates regular fruit consumption with lower risks of chronic diseases.

Fruits and vegetables also supply vitamins and minerals to the diet and are sources of phytochemicals that function as antioxidants, phytoestrogens, and anti-inflammatory agents. If you tend to get colds a lot or are sick more than usual, you probably are not eating enough fruits and vegetables.

I very rarely get sick anymore, but when I do I may act like a typical guy with a man cold, but I recover very quickly and I believe that has a lot to do with my diet and taking supplements.

Our bodies also need some fiber and we get that from vegetables and fruits. Yeah, you could eat some Bran Flakes (do they still make those?), or you could just eat more fruits and vegetables each day. I know the importance of fiber because my grandpa was always so focused on it. Fiber is linked to a lower incidence of cardiovascular disease and obesity. It didn't prevent my grandfather from having a heart attack, but his genetics had a little more to do with that and the fact that he didn't step a foot into a gym and he ate a meat and potatoes kind of diet his whole life. Wait, that means my genetics could get the best of me too. I guess that is why living a healthy lifestyle is so important to me. I know there are things at work that I can't control, but I can certainly do my best to adopt a healthy lifestyle to make sure my genetics don't get the best of me.

Try to eat something green with every meal. Make a smoothie with blueberries and greens. Put some spinach in your egg whites. Have some green beans with your chicken at lunch. Have some broccoli with your salmon at dinner. Have some fresh or dried fruit in between meals before lunch or for your mid-afternoon meal or snack. This advice has been around since we were kids, but it is still relevant today. Nothing has changed. The problem today is there is just too much new information when what we really need is a simple plan to live healthier. That simple plan is just going back to the basics.

Here are some simple ways to incorporate whole foods into your diet:

For Breakfast:

1. Replace sugary cereals with oatmeal topped with fresh fruit and walnuts.
2. Make smoothies with frozen fruit, leafy greens, and plain yogurt.
3. Put some spinach in your egg whites and eat whole grain toast.

For Lunch:

1. Choose brown rice instead of white rice for your carbs.
2. Make a spinach salad with almond slices and green peppers.
3. Make a quinoa bowl with your favorite protein.

For Dinner:

1. Make a stir-fry with fresh vegetables and free-range chicken strips.
2. Find some great soup recipes with legumes, beans, and kale.
3. Eat salmon with roasted broccoli and basmati rice.

The easiest way to start eating a whole foods diet is to start small. Add one whole foods meal per day. Replace processed snacks with fresh fruit, raw vegetables, and nuts. Once you start eating more and more whole foods you will crave them. You will feel more energy and lighter. You will start to feel healthier each day.

The Importance of Protein

There have been many new studies on how much protein you should have. I don't believe in fad diets like the Atkins diet, Paleo, or Keto. I have tried them all, and the hardest of all was Keto. I believe in Tony Horton's (founder of P90X) philosophy to be a flexitarian. Eat different things daily, balanced with the right amount of fat, protein, and carbs for your particular weight and chemistry. The one thing that helped me the most at age 51 to be the same weight I was when I was 18 is to have protein with every meal and eat most of my carbs earlier in the day. Pretty simple.

Protein is also extremely filling, which means that it will help you feel full sooner than fat or carbs (well, unless you eat a big pile of spaghetti. That is pretty darn filling). Digesting protein uses more energy than other foods, which can be really helpful when you are trying to lose weight or stay lean. Protein also helps maintain or build your muscle mass and the more of that you have, the more likely it is that your weight point will move down and stay there.

The idea that there is a 20-gram protein absorption limit has long been debunked. Protein should account for at least 30% of your calories. So, if your needs are 2,000 calories a day, that's 600 calories from protein.

The current recommendation is 1 g per pound of body weight split equally through three to five small meals/day for ideal protein synthesis (muscle building/repair) or about 30% of daily calories and then the rest from complex carbohydrates (40%) and fat (30%).

Current Weight: _____ × 1 = _____ Grams of Protein

Sample Protein-Focused Plan

Protein Amount

Pre-Workout:

Smoothie w/Protein 25 grams
Wild Blueberries 1 gram

Breakfast:

Egg Whites (4 oz) 20 grams
Avocado 2 grams
Spinach (1½ cups) 2 grams

Mid-Morning:

Almonds (1 oz) 7 grams
Hummus (1/3 cup) 7 grams

Lunch:

Chicken (6 oz) 42 grams
Quinoa (1/3 cup) 6 grams

Afternoon:

Greek Yogurt (5 oz) 15 grams
Granola (1 cup) 8 grams

Dinner:

Salmon (6 oz) 42 grams
Brown Rice (1/3 cup) 3 grams
Broccoli (1 cup) 7 grams

Early Evening:

Protein Shake 25 grams

***Day Total 212 grams**

*Getting the amount of protein that is suggested today is easier than you think. Tailor this plan to your weight and you will have a plan to get the amount of protein you need each day. This doesn't have to be what you eat every day, that would be boring. Switch things up, try new recipes, make stir-frys, find good soup recipes, get different spices or sauces for your proteins. Give yourself some grace if you slip up and eat 10 cookies. Have a cheat day each week where you can eat whatever you want.

Shopping List:

Spinach, Kale, Brussels sprouts, Broccoli, Blueberries, Raspberries, Avocados, Sweet potatoes, Red peppers, Carrots, and Cauliflower.

Proteins:

- Grass-fed, free-range beef.
- Organic, free-range poultry.
- Wild-caught Alaskan salmon or Pacific and Californian halibut.
- Plant-based meats.

Frozen Vegetables:

- Stir-fry veggie mix
- Tri-colored pepper strips
- Spinach
- Broccoli
- Cauliflower
- Brussels sprouts
- Edamame
- Peas

Frozen Fruits:

- Berries and cherries
- Strawberries
- Mangos
- Frozen fruit bars

Wise Health Tips:

- Sign up for a meal service like Factor, Home Chef, or Hello Fresh. I use Factor meals because they are ready to go with just two minutes in the microwave, and they have a ton of flavor and healthy options.
- Buy frozen wild blueberries and other fruits for smoothies so you don't always have to go to the grocery store to buy fruit that seems to be rotten before you can eat it.
- Divide your plate of food at each meal with 1/3 green vegetables, 1/3 high-quality protein, 1–3 tablespoons of high-quality fats (olive oil, hemp oil, etc.), and 1/3 nutrient-dense starch grain (brown rice, quinoa, lentils).
- Get a good plant-based protein powder, like Ka'Chava, Huel, or Momentous Essential (I have no affiliation with this brand).

HEALTH DECISION #4: CLEAN OUT YOUR PANTRY

Having junk food or processed food in your pantry is too tempting. We have become addicted to crap. Cool Ranch Doritos are oh-so good, but they have an addictive chemical. One of the first ingredients on the food's label is monosodium glutamate (MSG), which is an additive that's been known to increase appetite and make foods taste more appetizing. Oreos are no different. As it turns out, these things are as almost as addictive as both cocaine and morphine, according to a 2013 animal study. I'm not sure I believe that, but I know it's hard to eat just one. In the junk food business there's even a technical term they use called "bliss point." The bliss point describes the perfect combination of tastes and textures that makes a product nearly irresistible. These food technicians have discovered that the dopamine in our brain surges a lot more when properties like sweet and salty are put together in a combination. No wonder once I had a salted caramel latte, I craved one every day. Disclaimer: I don't drink a salted caramel latte every day. I drink two. Just kidding. I do like to have one as a treat on Sundays though before I make the kids' breakfast.

Cleaning your pantry will help you feel lighter, healthier, and more organized. When it comes to junk food, there are a few items that you may want to get rid of to improve your overall nutrition and set your environment up to give you a better chance to make good choices. Some items to remove from your pantry include sugary snacks like candy, cookies, and pastries, as well as salty snacks like chips and crackers. Also, highly processed foods like microwave popcorn, sugary cereals, and granola bars loaded with added sugars and artificial ingredients should be thrown in the trash. By eliminating these types of foods from your pantry, you can help create a healthier environment that supports your healthy lifestyle.

6 Food Items to Remove from Your Pantry

- Products with large amounts of added sugar or high-fructose corn syrup like soda, pop tarts, instant oatmeal, pancake syrup that is not pure maple, jams or jellies with high sugar, and white breads.
- Replace white flour with wheat flour, almond flour, or other healthy flour alternatives.
- Replace white instant rice with brown rice.
- Avoid processed and prepackaged food like chips, cheese puffs, Doritos, cookies, crackers, enriched pasta, and sugary cereals.
- Partially hydrogenated vegetable oil should be replaced with coconut oil, avocado oil, and olive oil.
- Avoid artificial flavor enhanced foods like ramen, canned soup with high sodium, packaged rice and pasta mixes, and salty snack mixes.

What to Stock in Your Pantry

Herbs and Spices:

- Himalayan or Celtic Sea Salt
- Black peppercorns
- Dried herbs: basil, oregano, Italian seasoning, rosemary, and thyme
- Dried spices: cumin, curry; ginger; turmeric; red pepper flakes; paprika; chili powder; cinnamon, Mexican spice blend, etc.

Condiments, Oils, and Other Ingredients:

- Extra virgin olive oil
- Extra virgin coconut oil
- Vinegars: apple cider, balsamic, red wine
- Coconut milk
- Salsa
- Olives

- Mustard
- Curry paste
- Marinara or tomato sauce
- Organic/non-GMO, reduced-sodium chicken, vegetable, and/or beef broths
- Hot sauce or Sriracha

Fruits and Vegetables:

- Dried fruits and raisins (without sulfites)
- Water-packed fruits (without sulfites)
- Sun-dried tomatoes, canned tomatoes, and tomato paste
- Bananas

Nuts, Nut Butters, and Seeds:

- Sesame seeds
- Pistachios
- Raw almonds, walnuts, cashews, and pecans
- Nut and seed butters (almond, sunflower, cashew, tahini)
- Chia seeds
- Hemp seeds
- Raw pumpkin seeds

Proteins/Carbs:

- Basmati, brown, and/or wild rice
- Quinoa (various colors)
- Gluten-free or regular oats
- Brown rice pasta

Beans/Legumes:

- Chickpeas
- Black and red beans

- Organic, reduced-sodium refried black or pinto beans
- Dried lentils

Baking:

- 55–70% dark chocolate chips, nibs, cocoa powder, and bars
- Whole grain or gluten-free, non-GMO pancake or waffle mix
- Gluten-free flours: oat, almond, coconut, all-purpose gluten-free blend
- Maple syrup or brown rice syrup
- Shredded unsweetened coconut
- Vanilla extract

Beverages:

- Green tea
- Herbal teas
- Unsweetened almond, rice, or coconut milk
- Coconut water

Wise Health Tip: Clean out your pantry today. Go shopping and, when you get home, put all the healthy things at eye level.

HEALTH DECISION #5: DRINK MORE THAN ENOUGH WATER

Drinking water has a ton of health benefits. We have all been told to drink more water. It helps to keep our bodies hydrated, regulates body temperature, and aids digestion. It also helps to flush toxins out of the body and keeps our skin healthy. Drinking enough water can also help with weight management and may prevent kidney stones and urinary tract infections.

To maintain good health, we should try to drink at least eight glasses of water each day. Most of us don't do that, and we are dehydrated, affecting our mood, concentration, and mental performance. Dehydration can also trigger headaches in some people. So, your headache yesterday could be a result of not drinking enough water.

One often-not-talked-about benefit of drinking enough water is the benefit on our joints. Water is essential in producing what is called synovial fluid. Think of it like oil for your joints. It's a lubrication liquid that reduces friction between the cartilage and tissues between our joints. This is super important if we want to be active as we age and our body starts to feel like the tin man from the Wizard of Oz.

Make It Easy

Drink two glasses of water when you wake up while the coffee is brewing and then drink a glass of water before each meal. This can help decrease your appetite and make you eat less, which can help with weight loss if that is your goal, but it also gets you closer to your goal of drinking eight glasses of water each day. If you eat five small meals per day and drink a glass of water each time, you will hit your goal easily for the day.

Wise Health Tip: Health-conscious people always carry a water bottle around to remind them to drink enough water each day. Get one.

HEALTH DECISION #6: DO YOGA, STRETCHING, AND MEDITATION

All right, I get it. You're not a Yogi or a monk. Neither am I, but I have grown to love yoga and meditation, and the benefits are even greater later in life, especially yoga. I just turned 51, and the two steel cables I have for my hamstrings are preventing me from touching my toes like I used to be able to do. Hell, I couldn't even get my fingertips past my mid-shins a couple of years ago until I incorporated some yoga into my life. Since I am not a Yogi, I do it as part of an exercise routine at my favorite fitness franchise. SPENGA is a group fitness facility that has a 60-minute workout that starts with 20 minutes of spin, then 20 minutes of strength, followed by 20 minutes of yoga. I love it. And the bonus is that I can almost touch my toes without bending my knees. Having two bulging disks in the lower back from lifting heavy weights in my twenties makes it all more crucial that I have flexibility. A lot of people don't realize that the majority of lower back problems are from tight hamstrings, and the rest is from having a weak core. SPENGA solves both by incorporating core exercises and yoga into everyday workouts. Having a strong core is not about having a six-pack; it is about balance. When you are out of balance, that is when you feel your back tweak when you bend over to pick up a sock.

Meditation

Meditation can help relieve stress and create peace in your mind. I never understood how to do it and felt I was awful at it. I remember the first time I incorporated meditation into my life. I used the Headspace app and found my mind wandering a lot. Maybe I do have ADD after all. However, after doing the guided lessons, I started to learn the purpose of meditation. It is not to turn off your thoughts, it's about noticing when you get off track with the meditation routine and start thinking of something about your day or that you are stressed about and redirecting yourself back to your breathing. When I started to meditate more and more, I got addicted to the way I felt at the end of those 10–15 minutes. I loved the way I felt when I opened my eyes. I felt peace and light. I felt less stressed. I felt open and ready to get on with my day.

Meditation forces you to pay more attention to your feelings, thoughts, and state of mind. It helps you with life. It helps you become more aware and intentional about how you communicate in life or how you react to situations. When you want to say something, you may wait before you say it. When you feel angry, you may delay your reaction for a few seconds or leave the room. When someone says something critical, you may stop taking things too personally. It allows you to control how you react to things. The old adage that "life is not what happens to you, but how you react" comes down to peace, and you get that from some meditation practice. When you can control how you react, life will be better and filled with fewer worries about things that don't really matter. Peace will allow you to focus on things that are important.

Stretching

As you age, your hamstrings become really tight and stiff and pull on your lower back muscles. Like I said earlier, most lower back problems are from tight hamstrings. I have found the easiest way to incorporate stretching into my day is to do some stretches while the coffee is brewing in the morning. Set a goal to touch your toes again one day, or at least get closer and closer to that goal.

If yoga isn't your thing, but you want some easy yoga poses to do without doing a 60-minute yoga routine, my favorite yoga moves are the pigeon pose and low lunge, which both help your hip flexors. If you cannot do the pigeon pose, substitute a reclining pigeon pose on your back. The cat/cow, sphinx pose, seated forward fold, and supine twist are also great yoga moves to help with flexibility and lower back pain and are fairly easy to do. I will not go into how to do these with long descriptions. Do a Google search on yoga stretches for lower back pain and incorporate these into your morning routine. All it takes is about 10–15 minutes.

Wise Health Tip: Stretch every day while your coffee is brewing.

HEALTH DECISION #7: EAT FOUR TO FIVE SMALL MEALS PER DAY

I grew up eating three meals a day because that is what we did in the eighties, but I was a picky eater, just like my son is now. When I was 13, I weighed about 72 pounds. I can still remember having to weigh ourselves in front of the science class for an experiment. The only kid who was close to my weight was the smallest kid in school, and he weighed about 78 pounds. I'm pretty sure they would never have a kid weigh themself in front of the entire classroom today. I got made fun of by the girls for being skinny and having no butt. It wasn't until I was about 15 that things changed for me. My voice went from a soprano to a low baritone almost overnight (yeah, I was a late bloomer), and I started lifting weights. I was about 130 pounds when I was 15, and by 16, I weighed about 165 lb. I read books on nutrition and followed a workout plan designed by Arnold Schwarzenegger that allowed me to pack on the muscle and finally have a butt. I could barely find jeans that fit by the time I was 17, because my thighs had gotten pretty big. Considering I used to have bird legs, that was a big accomplishment. Part of the nutrition plan was to eat four to five small meals daily and a ton of protein. To get the protein I needed each day, I bought a meal replacement called MegaMass 2,000. It had a whopping 2000 calories per serving and a ton of carbs, too. Goodbye six-pack, but hello, 19-inch arms.

When I turned 40 years old, I gained about 20 pounds. It was the heaviest I had ever been. My body fat was 18.5%, my cholesterol was Lipitor levels, and my pants were uncomfortably snug. I set a goal to lose 10 pounds, 2% of my body fat, and two inches off my waist in 30 days. I set a workout schedule for four days a week and committed to a program designed by a personal trainer. It worked, and I hit my 30-day goal and have adopted a health-conscious mindset into my life. Today, I am 51 and in the best shape of my life, well, minus the six-pack and 19-inch arms.

This was my food plan for 30 days:

Meal 1: 7:30 a.m. Half cup of oatmeal with bananas and 2/3 cup of egg whites.

Meal 2: 10 a.m. Protein shake with 8 oz water or almond milk, one scoop protein powder with a dash of cinnamon. Two rice cakes.

Meal 3: 12:30 p.m. 5 oz meat source – turkey, chicken, fish, or beef, ½ cup brown rice or sweet potato.

Meal 4: 3:30 p.m. Two handfuls of almonds, one RTD Lean Shake 25.

Meal 5: 6:00 p.m. 5 oz meat source, 1–2 cups green veggies – broccoli, beans or spinach, less than ½ cup carb source like brown rice or sweet potatoes.

Meal 6: Never past 8:30 p.m. If hungry on workout days and didn't get enough protein, I would eat two whole eggs with ½ cup eggs whites and ¼ cup cheese.

Most of you would look at this diet and go, "No way." I love spaghetti and pizza way too much. Well, eat the pizza. Have some spaghetti; just don't eat a whole pizza or a mound of pasta more than once a week. Or try making a cauliflower crust pizza or spaghetti with zucchini noodles. Both are actually really good and have a ton less carbs.

It's amazing what happens when you work out and eat healthily. Your body actually craves good, healthy food. When you don't exercise and eat unhealthy foods, your body craves junk. Eat small healthy meals, and you will not only feel better but also lose weight, increase your energy, and increase your overall health and well-being, not to mention your confidence will soar. I owe a lot of my confidence in life to working out and eating right.

Meal Planning and the Hunger Scale

Eating four or five meals per day allows you to get nutrition throughout the day and not overeat when you have a meal. So plan your meals and snacks, and don't wait until you are hungry. In my health and life coach training, I learned about the hunger scale. If you want to build healthy habits around food, what you eat is only part of the picture. You also have to look at how and when you eat. Are you eating when you're starving, or do you eat too much at once? If there was a hunger scale from 1 to 10 and 1 is just starting to notice hunger, 10 is feeling famished, start to plan for food when you are at a two or three on the hunger scale, and stop eating your food before you feel full. Most of us eat beyond fullness. If you eat four to five small meals per day you will do this naturally and not have to constantly think about where you are on the hunger scale.

So plan your meals and try to eat four to five smaller meals per day. This will prevent you from eating only when you are hungry, your food will have time to digest, and you won't overeat at each meal.

> **Wise Health Tip**: Put your extra small meals in a schedule on your phone with two alerts to remind you it is time to eat in between your main meals.

HEALTH DECISION #8: TAKE SOME SUPPLEMENTS

Most supplements are a complete waste of money. The companies that make them are just good at marketing, but there are some crucial supplements you should take. I always look at it this way: Would you rather spend $200 a month today to stay in better health or $2,000 per month down the road on prescription drugs? (They say the average 65-year-old is on between seven and ten prescription drugs.) If you are like me, I hate taking pills, so I try to find powders, drinkable supplements, or chewable pills. Plus, I have always found it hard to stay consistent having that many pills to take every day. I take an Olly multivitamin chewable, magnesium capsules, and a magnesium powder in my tea in the evening. I also take a liquid Omega-3 supplement in the morning with my breakfast as well as some vitamin D3 capsules which are easy to swallow because they are small and slippery.

1. **Multivitamins**

   A good multivitamin is one of the most important supplements we can take. We have heard it since we were young. Most of us don't get what we need by diet alone, so taking a high-quality multivitamin each day will help you get important vitamins like vitamin D, B12, B6, C, and E. An Olly chewable multivitamin or the Ultimate Multivitamin by Envitamin are two good options.

1. **Fish Oil**

   Fish oil provides the body with essential Omega-3 fatty acids, which are crucial to our health. Omega-3s help regulate blood pressure and immune function, support your mood, and promote muscle and joint health. You should try to supplement your diet with 500–900 mg of Omega-3 fatty acids through eating oily fish and a good Omega-3 supplement.

   Try having at least three servings of oily fish (like salmon, anchovies, and mackerel) per week. I don't know about you, but I have no interest in anchovies, but salmon cooked right is perfect. I have about seven different recipes for salmon. I don't even know what a mackerel is, but if you like them, eat them.

   If you are like me and hate the taste of fish oil, either take a good fish oil capsule to get your Omega-3 EPA/DHA or buy some Barlean's Mango Peach Smoothie Omega-3, which is dairy-free and sugar-free. Barlean's has 1,080 mg of Omega-3 and some vitamin D as well.

2. **Magnesium**

   Magnesium has more than 600 enzyme reactions in the body. They call magnesium a helper nutrient. It protects your blood vessels and improves insulin resistance. It also helps convert vitamin D into a form that helps the kidneys and liver metabolize it. Magnesium can also help with your stress and anxiety levels. Sounds pretty important to me. If you consume a lot of highly processed foods, have diabetes, have gastrointestinal conditions, or suffer from vitamin D deficiency, you may be most at risk of a magnesium deficiency.

Magnesium Tip: Try to get at least 400 mg of magnesium per day in the form of a capsule or powder. One of my favorite ways to get magnesium is in the form of a powder I can take at night as a hot tea. There are many options out there, but I use Nello SuperCalm. It also has 300 mg of organic KSM 66 Ashwagandha, 400 mg of L-Theanine, 100 mg of chelated magnesium glycinate, and 1,000 IU of vitamin D. I also take magnesium in the form of a capsule to get my 400 mg per day. Magnesium helps you sleep better and is essential to optimal health. With Nello, I get some magnesium and other important supplements to aid with focus and stress management.

3. **Vitamin D**

   Most of us get a less-than-optimal level of vitamin D. They say vitamin D is necessary for muscle strength, calcium absorption, healthy immune response, and normal blood pressure, so getting enough vitamin D is pretty darn important. It also helps with your attitude and seasonal blues.

   Living in Minnesota, I know I have had issues over the years with the seasonal blues. Vitamin D has helped me a ton in this department. I also would consider getting a 10,000 Lux Sunlight Lamp to help with getting the feeling that sunlight gives us.

   Vitamin D Tip: Take at least 2,000 IU of vitamin D a day throughout the year and increase your vitamin D intake to 4000 IU in the fall to prepare for the winter season. This will help you with the lack of vitamin D you get from sunlight during those short gray days in the winter.

4. **Probiotics**

We digest and absorb nutrients through the gut, and probiotics are beneficial bacteria that help the gut work better. When I first learned about probiotics, I thought, you want me to put what down my throat into my belly? You want me to swallow bad bacteria? That sounds disgusting, but maintaining a balance between the "good" and the "bad" bacteria in the gut is important for overall health. They basically fight off the less friendly kinds of bacteria and can boost your immunity. You can get probiotics by eating yogurt, sauerkraut, kefir, and miso, but taking a supplement may be your best bet to balance the bacteria in your gut. Just be aware that not all probiotics are equal. Because of all the talk and chatter about probiotics, every nutrition company under the sun is making its version of a probiotic. I found the best ones to be ones that require refrigeration. Ask your doctor or nutritionist what brands are the most effective.

Wise Health Tip: Take your supplements with a designated meal or before bed. Make it a ritual.

HEALTH DECISION #9: COLD PLUNGE

I just started cold plunging, and I can tell you the first time I dipped my warm, cozy body into water so cold (42 degrees F) that it made my feet feel like they would shatter when I got out. Sounds fun, right? But before you run away screaming, let me tell you why cold plunging might be the coolest thing you can do for your health (pun intended).

Benefit #1: Instant Awakening

Forget coffee. If you want to wake up faster, try a cold plunge. It's like hitting the reset button on your brain, except instead of using your finger, you're using your entire body. Your whole body feels awakened. You will feel a tingle all over your body after you get out.

Benefit #2: Inflammation Reduction

Cold water immersion can reduce inflammation by constricting blood vessels and decreasing metabolic activity. This can help muscle recovery after exercise and may alleviate symptoms of some inflammatory conditions.

Benefit #3: Mood Boost

Ever seen a grumpy person jump into freezing water? No, because it's impossible to stay grumpy when you're busy gasping for air and wondering why you thought this was a good idea. But the fact is, the rush of endorphins that follows a cold plunge can lift your mood.

Benefit #4: Improved Circulation

Cold water forces your blood to move faster. This improved circulation can lead to better overall health.

The Science Behind Cold Plunging

Here are some of the other physiological effects and potential benefits of cold plunging:

1. **Vasoconstriction and Vasodilation**
   When you enter cold water, your blood vessels constrict (vasoconstriction) to redirect blood flow to vital organs. After leaving the cold water, your blood vessels dilate (vasodilation). This process can improve circulation and potentially strengthen blood vessels over time.

2. **Norepinephrine Release**

Cold exposure triggers the release of norepinephrine, a hormone and neurotransmitter. This can lead to increased alertness and focus and may have mood-boosting effects. Some studies suggest it might even help with depression and anxiety.

3. **Brown Fat Activation**

Cold exposure activates brown adipose tissue, also known as "brown fat." Unlike white fat, brown fat burns calories to generate heat. Regular cold exposure might increase the amount and activity of brown fat, potentially aiding in weight management.

4. **Immune System Boost**

Some research suggests that regular cold exposure might stimulate the immune system. It may increase the production of white blood cells and other immune system components.

5. **Hormetic Stress**

Cold plunging is a form of hormesis – a beneficial stress that can make the body more resilient. This mild stress can trigger adaptive responses in the body, potentially improving overall health and stress tolerance.

6. **Increased Metabolism**

The body burns extra calories to maintain core temperature in cold water. While the effect is temporary, regular cold exposure might lead to a slight increase in your overall metabolic rate.

7. **Improved Sleep**

Some people report improved sleep quality after cold plunging, possibly due to the regulation of core body temperature and the release of endorphins.

It's important to note that while promising research exists, some of the benefits of cold plunging are still being studied. Individual responses can vary, and it's always wise to consult with a healthcare professional before starting any new health regimen, especially one involving extreme temperatures.

Cold Plunging Tip: Work your way up to three minutes of cold plunges at 42 degrees F. Buy some neoprene booties and keep your hands out for the entire plunge. The first 15–20 seconds are the toughest, but stay committed. Three minutes is all you need to get the majority of the benefits.

HEALTH DECISION #10: IMPLEMENT INTERMITTENT FASTING

I don't think I could ever do a three-day fast. I know the benefits, but it sounds like three days of hell. But intermittent fasting is something I can do, and the benefits are big. Intermittent fasting has gained a lot of attention lately, and for good reason. It's a simple but powerful approach to eating that can have some great benefits for your health and well-being. Here are a few key advantages:

1. **Weight management:** By limiting your eating window, you may naturally consume fewer calories, which can help with weight loss or maintenance.
2. **Improved insulin sensitivity:** Fasting periods can give your body a break from processing glucose, potentially improving insulin function.
3. **Cellular repair:** During fasting, your body may kick-start processes that remove damaged proteins and other cellular components.
4. **Brain health:** Some studies suggest intermittent fasting might support brain health and potentially reduce the risk of neurodegenerative diseases.
5. **Simplicity:** Many people find it easier to stick to than traditional diets since it focuses on when you eat rather than what you eat.

6. **Increased energy:** Once you adjust to the eating pattern, many people report feeling more energetic and focused during fasting periods.

Intermittent Fasting Tips

1. **Start gradually:** Begin with a shorter fasting window, like 12 hours, and slowly increase it as your body adjusts.
2. **Stay hydrated:** Drink plenty of water during fasting periods to help manage hunger and maintain energy levels.
3. **Choose a method that fits your lifestyle:** Popular approaches include 16/8 (16 hours fasting, 8 hours eating), 5:2 (eating normally for five days, restricting calories on two days), or eat-stop-eat (24 hours fasting once or twice a week). My favorite and the most doable for me is the 16/8 approach.
4. **Plan your meals:** During eating windows, focus on nutrient-dense, balanced meals to ensure proper nutrition.
5. **Be mindful of your eating window:** Avoid late-night eating, if possible, as it can disrupt sleep and digestion.
6. **Listen to your body:** If you feel unwell or overly hungry, you can adjust your fasting schedule or have a small snack.
7. **Get enough sleep:** Good sleep can help regulate hunger hormones and make fasting easier.
8. **Exercise smartly:** Light exercise during fasting can be beneficial, but intense workouts are better saved for normal eating days.
9. **Be patient:** It may take a few weeks for your body to adapt fully to the new eating pattern.

Fasting Tip: Try doing a 16/8 (16 hours fasting, 8 hours eating) intermittent fast once a week and work your way up to twice a week over 90 days. I usually only do intermittent fasting once or twice per week on non-workout days.

Summary of Health Decisions to Live a Richer Life

These are just some of the top health decisions to consider implementing. You can't do them all at once, but implementing some of them slowly over a year will greatly impact your health and longevity. They are in order of importance. The first decision is to adopt a healthy living mindset. The next decision is to work out or be active. Start with long walks; if you aren't used to going to the gym, incorporate some workouts at home or 15-minute HIIT routines into your week. Clean out your pantry. Eat smaller, more frequent meals. Don't eat after dinner, and drink plenty of water. Start eating more protein, less bad carbs, and take some supplements.

In the first 90 days, with the health goals part of your 90-Day Health and Wealth Action Plan, do the easy things, then introduce new things every 90 days.

Here is an example of a plan to become healthier over your first year:

First 90-Day Period:

1. Buy a 24 oz water bottle and drink two bottles per day.
2. Clean out your pantry and stop eating processed food.
3. Walk every day or do something active.

Second 90-Day Period:

1. Buy fresh produce and some plant-based protein powders.
2. Eat smaller meals four or five times per day.
3. Incorporate two 15-minute HIIT routines each week.

Third 90-Day Period:

1. Buy some of the suggested supplements and take them with a designated meal.

2. Do some yoga, stretching, and consider mediation.
3. Incorporate two days of strength training in addition to your two days of HIIT routines.

Fourth 90-Day Period:

1. Eat greens with every meal.
2. Do some intermittent fasting twice per week on your non-workout or lower activity days.
3. Try a cold plunge if your gym has one, or buy a portable one for your garage.

One year from now, you will have ingrained a healthy lifestyle into your life, which will become your new standard. You will feel better, have more energy, and become addicted to being active. You will be on your way to living a better life in the health department, and health is wealth.

Summary of Life, Wealth, and Health Decisions

If you follow this set of life, wealth, and health principles, you will be on your way to living a richer life. Whether you want financial independence or financial freedom, better health, or a more fulfilling life, an investment in knowledge always pays the best interest, as Benjamin Franklin said. But knowledge without action won't get you the permanent changes you are looking for. The next step is to develop a plan of action to create a positive, lasting change in your life that becomes part of who you are. You have to believe a better life is possible for you and make a commitment to yourself anchored with deep inspiration and a vision of the future. Now you need a plan to start living that richer life each day.

CHAPTER NINE

THE 7 STEPS TO BETTER HEALTH, MORE WEALTH, AND A RICHER LIFE

You have learned a lot in this book. You have learned that you have to shift your identity and how you view yourself if you want lasting change in any part of your life. You have learned that you need to set new standards for your life, wealth, and health. You have learned the importance of personal growth and have been given the top 10 life, wealth, and health decisions I believe can help you live a richer life. Now it is time to put it all into action. There are 7 Steps to achieve better health, more wealth, and a richer life. The first step for achieving your most important goals is deciding what you truly want.

STEP 1: Decide What You Want for Your Life, Wealth, and Health.

What do you really want for your life? Do you want financial security, financial independence, or true financial freedom? Do you want to be healthier than you were 10 years ago? Do you want to make a bigger difference to those you care about? Do you want a better relationship with your spouse? Do you want to bring more joy into your life? Do you want to be more present and enjoy the moments and all the experiences that life has in front of you?

What is most important to you now, and what do you want your life to look like 10 years from now? Deciding what you want is the first step. Then, you need an intentional plan to live a life by design.

You need to be specific. Most people don't ever get what they want because they don't know what they want. If you have trouble knowing what you want, try describing your ideal life. Use the following questions to guide you.

Describe Your Ideal Life

1. If your work life and career were ideal, what would they look like?
2. If your family life were ideal, what would it look like, and what one discipline would help you the most to make it a reality?
3. If your health were perfect in every way, what would that look like?
4. If your financial situation were ideal today, what would that look like? How much would be in your bank account? In savings and investments?
5. What would a successful life look like to you?
6. What skills would help you develop and realize more of your goals?
7. If you could be completely disciplined in one area, what would have the greatest positive impact on your life?
8. What impact would you be making for others if you met your goals long-term?
9. What would you do with your spare time if you had more energy, better health, and greater freedom?

One of the things that will become vital when setting goals for yourself is finding clarity. There is a direct relationship between the level of clarity you have about who you are and what you want and just about everything you accomplish in life. It is also very important to set personal goals. They must be goals that you set for yourself rather than some goals that someone else sets for you or that you want to reach to please someone else in your life. For goal-setting to be the most effective, you must be somewhat selfish about what you really want for yourself. This doesn't mean you won't do things for those you care about or be selfish with everything else in your life; it just means setting goals for your life will start with you and what you truly desire.

Ask yourself what you must do to create your richer life, three, five, or 10 years from now. Start thinking about "How" you can achieve the things in your life rather than "Can" you achieve those things. Don't focus so much on the future that you get so anxious that you can't enjoy each day. Focus on the things you need to do to achieve your future self today in the present. Don't give up because of a short-term goal not met. Give yourself some grace, especially in the first 90 days and over the course of the first year of change and improvement. Don't give up if you don't reach that year-end goal. Keep your sights on your long-term vision with daily actions. You will get there one day at a time.

Jim Rohn often said, "When you know what you want, and want it bad enough, you will find a way to get it." You have to have enough reasons to reach your goals. The more reasons you have to succeed, the more of a pull you have from the future. More reasons lead to more commitment. More commitment leads to positive feelings. Positive feelings lead to more action. More action leads to better results.

Staying motivated and enthusiastic is what ignites us to take action and work toward our goals. But how do we stay motivated every day? How do we maintain our ambition and drive? These questions have been on my mind ever since I started my career after college. I often find myself wanting to succeed but struggling to stay motivated. It can be frustrating when you have the desire to take action but lack the inner strength and motivation to do so.

To build and sustain your motivation, you simply need to find enough reasons for success. You have to have enough reasons to want more – to be more. This means finding out what matters to you and what actions would bring benefits and improvement to your life and the lives of those you care about. Think deeply and discover your real goals in life. What will give you the most satisfaction 10 years from now if you achieve them?

A helpful exercise to decide what you really want and why is to take out a sheet of paper and write out all the reasons you want to achieve financial freedom, better health, or better relationships. Start by writing, "Why I want to reach my financial goals," and list as many reasons as you can in 15 minutes. Then take 15 minutes to write out all the reasons why better health is important to you. Then do the same for your relationships, your career, or anything else you want to get clear on.

Live in Alignment With Your Core Values

Look around your house. Most of the things you have are not necessarily things you need, but they are things you want. We have a lot of things we don't need, but we have them because we have a desire and want to have them. If you want more success in your life, you have to really want it. If you want more energy or better health in your life, you have to create it. Many of us work hard on the outside to achieve goals we think we want, only to find that we get no satisfaction from them. Make sure what you really want is in line with your core values. Living in alignment with your true values and ideals is one of the keys to long-term happiness. Where do you want to spend your money and your time? What do you value most? What is most important to you?

So what is important to you:

1. What Do You Want for Your Health?

One year from now: _____

Three years from now: _____

10 years from now: _____

2. What Do You Want for Your Wealth?

One year from now: _____

Three years from now: _____

10 years from now: _____

3. What Do You Want for Your Life?

One year from now: _____

Three years from now: _____

10 years from now: _____

Example of knowing what you want:

Your Health:

One year from now: I want to lose two inches off my waist and adopt a healthy lifestyle.

Three years from now: I want to have endless energy and play pickleball two to three days a week without being tired and sore.

10 years from now: I want to be able to travel, play with my grandkids, and not have to take any prescription drugs.

Your Wealth:

> One year from now: I want to be able to save and invest 20% of my income for the future.

> Three years from now: I want to be on a path toward financial independence.

> 10 years from now: I want to have a net worth of $1.5 million.

Your Life:

> One year from now: I want to spend more quality time with family and friends and try new things.

> Three years from now: I want to be able to travel two or three times a year.

> 10 years from now: I want to make a difference with the causes I care about and have a strong relationship with my partner.

Designing Your Life With the End in Mind

Do you want just to have life happen to you, or do you want to make things happen in your life? Jim Rohn said, "We are trapped by either the regret of the past or the routine of the present. We are so busy with the routine of the present that we don't give much thought to designing a better future." If we could only have a glimpse of our better future. If you design a life, you will create a pull from the future that will act like a magnet. It will pull you through all kinds of situations, obstacles, and downtime.

When you know what you want, rate your motivation on a scale from 1 to 10, where 1 is not motivated and 10 is very motivated. Then ask yourself the following questions: What would your life be like if you got the things you want? What would change for you personally and financially? Next ask yourself the question, if you got what you wanted and it changed things financially and personally for you, how would that make you feel?

Whatever that feeling is, it will be what you need to focus on to fuel your motivation toward living this richer life.

When you decide what you want for yourself and your life, ask the simple question, "Is it big enough." Is it big enough for what you truly desire? What we think we want is usually just an impulse on how we see ourselves today. After going through these seven steps, you will see yourself better, and you will have a vision for your life that is bigger than you right now. Because whether you believe it or not right now, you have so much more that you are capable of. So much more to give. So much more to become. You deserve something more for your life, but first, you have to want it.

Summary of Deciding What You Want for Your Life, Wealth, and Health

Knowing what you want is the first step. If you don't know what you want, you won't be able to set clear goals. When you look at your list of all the things you want, get rid of any fake goals or things that you know are not that important to you. Focus on the things that you want to improve now or within the next 90 days. The next step is finding the why behind your why.

STEP 2:   Find Your Why Behind the Why.

Finding your why is easy. Finding the why behind your why is a little bit more challenging, but it is necessary to keep your inspiration long-term so that you can act in your best interests. Your choices are more meaningful when you connect them to your deepest why. You've got to want something and know why you want it, or you'll end up giving up too easily. Your why can't be about making a fortune, buying a bigger house, or having fancy things. If you think you will be happy with a big pile of money as your main goal in life, you will most likely be just richer, not happier and more fulfilled. Identifying the why behind your why is a crucial step to living a richer life. What truly motivates you is what will fuel your passion, keep your enthusiasm high even when you have roadblocks, and be the thing that keeps you going. Your why behind your why is a deeper reason for why you want something in your life.

If you having trouble finding your why behind your why, "The 5 Why Method" is a great tool to help you find it. It was created by an inventor named Sakichi Toyoda to help engineers find the root cause of a problem and has been taught in schools all over the world. You first begin with something you want, then ask why you want it and keep asking why five more times until you find the why behind your why.

What do you want to do or achieve and why do you want it? Write your answer then ask why. Keep writing an answer until you get to the root why or the why behind the why. Do this exercise with your health, your career, your family relationships, and your wealth or financial situation.

Your Why Behind Your Why Is What Will Keep You Inspired Long-Term

"What will your moment be? When will you start to see everything differently, what will your moment be"
– "What Will Your Moment Be?" Brian David Band

To improve your health, build a successful career, or build your wealth, taking the time to find the why behind your why can help you stay committed and energized as you work toward your goals. You first need to understand your why for everything you do. Then it becomes easier to find your why behind your why. Having a clear understanding of the why behind your why is crucial for staying motivated and inspired over the long term. It's not enough to know what you want to achieve; you must also understand the deeper reasons why you're pursuing those goals. By connecting with your deeper why, you can stay focused and driven even when faced with obstacles or setbacks.

Simon Sinek is a world-renowned author, motivational speaker, and marketing consultant well-known for his philosophy of starting with "why" to achieve success. In his popular TED Talk, Simon emphasizes the importance of understanding your "why" and how it can help you achieve your goals in life and business. According to Simon, knowing your "why" can help you make better decisions, inspire others, and ultimately lead to greater fulfillment and success. So, if you're looking to unlock your full potential and achieve success in your personal and professional life, it's worth taking the time to discover your "why" and then understanding your why behind your why.

Examples of Identifying Your Why and Your Why Behind Your Why

1. My why for my wealth is to be on a path to achieve true financial freedom.

   My why behind my why when it comes to my wealth is to give myself and my family all the opportunities to live a richer life filled with more experiences and make a difference in the lives of those I care about and the causes that are important to me.

2. My why for my health is to be fit and in shape.

   My why behind my why when it comes to my health is to be healthy and fit long into my 60s and 70s so I can see my kids get married and become successful, productive adults, travel the world, and have the energy to play with my grandkids.

3. My why for my life is to live life to the fullest.

   My why behind my why when it comes to my life is to leave a lasting impact on those I know and don't know, have strong, deep connections, and be remembered. People won't remember what you said or did; they will remember how you made them feel. I want to look back at my life and know I made something of it. I found more meaning, made a difference, and created amazing experiences and memories for my family. I want to be there for all my kids' milestones in life and instill the principles of living a richer life so that they can look back at their life and be as proud as I am.

Summary of Finding Your Why Behind Your Why

Knowing your why is fairly easy, but understanding the why behind your why is a bit more challenging. Knowing the why behind your why is necessary to keep you motivated long-term to achieve everything you want with your health, wealth, and life. The next step is to develop new standards that will become part of who you are. That will become your new default.

MOMENTOUS DECLARATION #9

I keep all my reasons close because they are the foundation of positive feelings that lead to more action and better results.

STEP 3:   Develop Life, Wealth, and Health Standards.

The first part of this book gave you a lot of life, health, and wealth decisions to consider for living a richer life. Many of them need to become your new standards. Not all at once, but over time. You may never become a cold plunger or do intermittent fasting, but you could start eating healthier or drinking enough water each day. You may not be able to put away 20% or 30% of your income today, but you can start by paying yourself 5% at first. You may not be able to fix your marriage or friendships, but you can start being intentional about the actions you take each day to improve those relationships. What does your future hold? Your current actions are creating and shaping your future. If you want to know what your future holds, look to your actions; they are the best predictors of your future. Your actions tell the story. Your actions are a reflection of your current standards.

To live a richer life, you have to set the bar higher. You have to create new standards for your life, your wealth, and your health. When you have standards, you have commitment. These new standards need to become "MUSTS." A lot of our issues around money come down to the standards we have set for ourselves. This goes for our personal relationships as well as our health.

What Exactly Is a Standard?

A standard is the thing that we have become "okay" with. It's the thing that we have learned to tolerate in our lives, and it's what you consider to be the "norm." Did you know that you always get your standard? We don't always get what we want or desire, but we will get our standard. You and I are where we are today because of what we tolerate. The only way to experience a different life than what you are experiencing right now is to raise your standards. So, how can you change or raise your standards? In order to raise your standard, you have to become disgusted with your current standard to the point of saying, "Enough is enough."

For lasting change, you need to change your standard for yourself, not for a period of time, but for the new you. It's the only thing that will create lasting change. What does it mean to raise your standards? It's when you turn your shoulds into musts. The things that used to be your "should do" need to change to "must do." You do your should dos when they are convenient, when it's comfortable, when it goes your way.

I remember my tennis coach in high school had an expression every time he heard us say, "I should have gone up to the net more" or "I should have been more patient." He'd say, "If you have a handful of shit in one hand and one hand full of should've, could've, and would've in another, which weighs more? The shit, because should'ves, could'ves, and would'ves don't add up to shit."

Question: If something is a must, not for other people but a must for you, do you find a way to get it done? The answer is YES.

Your "MUST" Is Your New Standard

Our current physique is a reflection of our current physical standard. It shows up in your rituals. You have different rituals, certain things you do, if you MUST have your body look a certain way, versus I should, or I'd like to, or I want to.

Our current financial situation is a result of our money or wealth standard. We all want more wealth or money but are not committed as much as we should be with a must. We may not be doing the things necessary to reach our long-term goals because we haven't made them a must or a priority.

Your current income is a result of your standard. In order to raise your standards, you have to change the way you view yourself. Our self-perception and identity were mostly shaped by the feedback that our parents, friends, and teachers gave us growing up. As adults, they are shaped by our coworkers and bosses. The truth is that we cannot consistently act in a manner that is inconsistent with how we view ourselves.

Most of us set our standards according to our environment. If we are around people who don't take care of themselves, we will eventually lower our standards. If we have junk food in the house, we have not committed to a healthy lifestyle standard. If we don't pay ourselves first, we haven't set our financial goals as a new standard.

Why is it that someone can say, "I want to get in shape this year," and for a while, they do; however, something happens over time. They go back to their old ways and get discouraged. The answer is they didn't change their identity. They still saw themselves as a person who was not fit, didn't exercise, and ate the wrong foods. Instead, they have to view themselves as someone who exercises and eats the right foods. You learned about this in Chapter 1 on transforming your self-image and how it is crucial to create lasting change.

Find someone doing well and model yourself after them. The people directly around you shape who you are. They shape your future. You've probably heard this before, "Show me your friends, and I'll show you your future." Study the wealthy and create wealthy habits. Get things done, because they are absolute "MUSTS."

What Will You No Longer Accept or Put Up With?

Life gives you what you ask for. What are you asking for in your life? What don't you want to accept anymore? What will you no longer put up with?

When it comes to the things you will no longer accept in your life, they might be things like, you will no longer accept feeling broke, being a mediocre spouse, not being present and engaged with your family, or putting your career before your family.

When it comes to the things you will no longer put up with, it may be things like short-term satisfaction over long-term gains, not putting away money each month to build your wealth, not being able to have money to spend on birthdays or Christmas, not being healthy, being lazy, or not striving to get better every day.

So what will you no longer accept or put up with? Write them down:

1. _____
2. _____
3. _____

What Things Do You Aspire to Become?

When it comes to the things you aspire to become, they may include being a loving and engaged spouse, a great role model for your kids, a difference maker with your favorite causes, or a generous person.

What things do you aspire to become? Write them down:

1. _____
2. _____
3. _____

What Actions Do You Need to Take to Align with Your New Standards?

What are the actions you need to take today and over the next 90 days to improve your health, your career or business, and your relationship to align with what you won't accept, what you won't put up with, and what you aspire to become? To align your actions with your new standards or values, you may need to commit to truly eating healthy, working out three or four days per week, going on walks with your family, focusing on being more present with your kids, setting up an account away from easy access so you can start building an emergency fund, starting to pay yourself first, or reading 30 minutes a day of motivational content.

What actions do you need to take to align with your new standards? Write them down:

1. _____
2. _____
3. _____

If you want to make better decisions, you need to know your values and standards. You need to learn from your mistakes. You need to ask for help if you are unsure. You need to know what you want and why you want it. You need to have a compelling vision for your life so that every decision you make is centered around what is most important to you and what you want for your future. Whatever decisions you are faced with today, you can choose to go down a different path. A path that leads to a richer, more fulfilling life. It is your choice. If you want lasting change you need to set new standards and first start making the right choice the easy choice.

For wealth building, this means:

- Setting up automated savings for emergencies and the future.
- Unsubscribing from shopping newsletters.
- Having a 24-hour rule for any purchase over $100.

For health, this means:

- Keeping running shoes by your front door or workout clothes by your bed.

- Keeping healthy food at eye level in your fridge and pantry.
- Going to bed at the same time every night.

For your life, this means:

- Focusing on the three As for your most important relationships.
- Reading or listening to something positive every day.
- Practicing gratitude daily.

Sometimes all we have to do to find more success in our life is walk down another street. There is a Y in the road. You can go to the left, which is the road you have been on in the past, or you can take a new road with a clear path to a richer life. You get to choose.

To get what we truly want, we have to direct our focus on the right path. That road is different from the one you have been down before, and it will feel uncomfortable at first, but it is the one that will take you to where you want to go. Many of us have bigger visions of something better, but most of us don't know truly what we want. We tend to get caught up in our current situation and what is not working, and we get stuck there. The reason this happens time after time is because of the simple rule that whatever we focus our energy on, we get more of it.

New standards won't happen overnight. While you are taking action to become a new version of yourself, focus on the process and keep all your reasons close. There are a lot of self-development books that recommend you create some affirmations to help you work toward new habits that become standards. The problem with most affirmations is that they are not based in truth and sometimes they make you feel like an imposter. If you want to make some affirmations to help remind you of the person you want to become, the health and financial goals you want to achieve, or the relationships you want to have with your family or spouse, use the words "I am in the process." This will be more impactful for you, because they are based in the truth that you are in the process of working to become better, healthier, or wealthier. Here are some examples of "in the process" affirmations:

Financial Affirmations

- I am working toward having $100k in a taxable investment account.
- I am in the process of making enough to have an extra $2,000 per month to use for experiences and travel.
- I am in the process of being free from debt, except for my mortgage.
- I am in the process of building my wealth by putting away 20% of my income.

Personal Affirmations

- I am in the process of having a healthy and positive marriage by following the three As each day.
- I am in the process of becoming an exceptional role model for my children.
- I am in the process of being present and engaged when I am at home.
- I am in the process of becoming more positive by reading and listening to self-development material.

Health Affirmations

- I am in the process of being in perfect health and physical condition by working out five or six days per week.
- I am in the process of becoming a health-conscious person by cleaning out my pantry and eating more whole foods.
- I am in the process of becoming more flexible by stretching or doing short yoga routines each day.

Setting new standards is a process. It starts with getting clear on what you want, what you will no longer put up with and what actions you will take to make these new standards eventually part of who you are. So, set new standards for your life, health, and wealth, and you will be on your way to living a richer life. The next step is creating a vivid vision of what your future would look like 10 years from now if you lived a values-based life centered around achieving what you truly want for your health, your wealth, and your life.

MOMENTOUS DECLARATION #10

I will focus on opportunities, not obstacles, because I have goals I "must" achieve.

MOMENTOUS DECLARATION #11

I am committed to changing my current situation for my wealth and health by setting new standards for myself personally and professionally.

STEP 4:   Create a 10-Year Vision of Your Richer Life.

Creating a vision for your life is powerful because seeing things in your mind's eye and visualizing them can create a pull toward a better future. Most people don't do this step because it takes a lot of work to write out a compelling vision. To quote the band Switchfoot, "We were meant to live for so much more. Have we lost ourselves, somewhere we live inside, somewhere we live inside?" John Wooden once said, "Don't let what you can't do interfere with what you can do." We are meant to live at our highest potential. Many of us have lost ourselves or have yet to find our highest selves. Just know this, it's there.

Close your eyes and visualize where you want to be 10 years from now. It is time to create your 10-year vision.

CREATING A 10-YEAR MOMENTOUS VISION OF YOUR RICHER LIFE

1. **Write your vision out in the form of a story.**

   Your vision should get you excited and read like a story that ignites you each day to take action. It should be vivid and maybe even give you goosebumps when you read it.

2. **Share it with others.**

   Sharing your vision increases your commitment to it. When you tell someone else what you want for your life, you feel more responsible for acting.

3. **Keep your vision close.**

   Put your compelling vision on your phone with pictures. Review it at least once a week and update it every time you discover ways to make it more vivid and meaningful to you.

4. **Take action on your vision.**

   Create a 90-day plan and take action each day on the things related to your vision for your life 10 years from now. If you spend the minutes each day doing the things you must do, the future will take care of itself.

5. **Live with intention.**

   At the end of each day, take a few minutes to reflect on the progress that you made today. Did it move you forward, or was it filled with things unrelated to your vision? What action will you take tomorrow?

THE 10-YEAR MOMENTOUS VISION FOR YOUR LIFE

Your Momentous Vision should read like a story. It should be vivid and detailed. It should get you excited. Describe what you envision your life to look like 10 years from now. Don't worry if the first draft of your vision is not perfect. Once you have the first draft, revise it until it feels authentic and excites you when you read it. Once it is complete, put it in a note on your phone, add pictures to make it even more compelling, and read it often.

If you want to make it even more powerful, record it, save it to your phone, and listen to it once per week on Sundays or at least once per month.

Most self-development books have exercises like this, but most people don't take the time to create a plan or vision for their lives. This is your chance to create a compelling vision that will pull you to live life by design each day.

To give you an idea of how your 10-year vision should be, I have shared my 10-year vision for my life after this framework. Once you are done with yours, share it with someone you care about, whether that is your spouse or a good friend.

Here is the framework for creating your vision of what you want your life to look like 10 years from now:

YOUR 10-YEAR MOMENTOUS VISION

PERIOD ENDING: _____
DESCRIBE THE CLOSENESS OF YOUR FAMILY, YOUR FINANCIAL SITUATION, AND YOUR HEALTH AND WELL-BEING:

_____

_____

WHERE DO YOU LIVE? WHAT KIND OF HOUSE? AS YOU LOOK OUT INTO YOUR BACKYARD, WHAT DO YOU SEE? WHAT DO YOU SMELL? HOW DO YOU FEEL?

_____

_____

WHAT PHOTOS ARE FRAMED ON THE WALL OF YOUR HOME WITH PLACES YOU HAVE GONE? WHAT EXPERIENCES HAVE YOU HAD? WHAT HAVE BEEN SOME OF YOUR FAVORITE MOMENTS?

_____

_____

WHAT HAS YOUR CAREER ALLOWED YOU TO DO OUTSIDE OF YOUR JOB? WHAT GOALS HAVE YOU MET WITH YOUR CAREER?

_____

_____

WHAT IMPACT ARE YOU MAKING IN THE LIVES OF YOUR FAMILY, FRIENDS, AND / OR CAUSES?

_____

_____

WHAT PASSIONS ARE YOU FOLLOWING? WHAT NEW OR OLD HOBBIES ARE YOU DOING?

_____

_____

WHAT ARE YOU DOING TO BRING JOY INTO YOUR LIFE?

_____

_____

HOW MUCH TIME ARE YOU TAKING OFF? DO YOU OWN ANY VACATION PROPERTIES? DO YOU HAVE A CABIN OR LAKE PLACE?

_____

_____

FOR WHAT CAUSES ARE YOU MAKING A DIFFERENCE, AND WHAT ARE YOU ABLE TO GIVE EACH YEAR?

_____

_____

WHEN YOU GO TO BED, YOU SLEEP SOUNDLY KNOWING:

_____

_____

MY 10-YEAR MOMENTOUS VISION

End Date: December 2034

My family is financially secure, healthy and fit, and close emotionally. We always have $40–50k in our money-market account for emergencies. We walk, bike, play cards, or shoot pool as a family after dinner, and talk about our roses and thorns for the day. I reached my net worth goal and continue to pursue the things I am passionate about while continuing to work with my top clients. I play pickleball two or three days a week in various competitive leagues and open play groups and have met some amazing people who have become close friends. I also spend my free time volunteering with the kids in various organizations in my community. I speak yearly at high schools in the Twin Cities, teaching teens how to make better wealth decisions through the Momentous Wealth Academy.

We live in a beautiful home on 1.5 acres with a three-season porch, four-car garage, and six bedrooms. The backyard has a beautiful cobblestone patio with plenty of seating for entertaining, a fire pit for family bonfire nights and outdoor movies, and an eight-person hot tub. I put in a pickleball court in five years ago, and neighborhood friends come every Thursday night for matches, drinks, and good conversations.

We frequently host dinner parties with our neighbors and good friends, where everyone congregates in our spacious kitchen, which has a large, beautiful granite island that opens up to the family room. Large dark wood beams line the living room ceiling, and light hardwood floors cover the main floor. The master bedroom has a large bathroom with white marble tile, a chandelier, a large walk-in shower, a clawfoot tub, and a vanity area.

I am in the best shape of my life and work out six days a week in our beautiful home gym, which has hardwood floors, a complete dumbbell rack, stretching mats, and a zen meditation area with a wall waterfall.

We have Music Mondays as a family in my professional studio, where we play along to classic songs and make music of our own. I am so proud of the musicians my kids have become.

When I am not spending time with my family, I spend some of my free time doing creative things I am passionate about. I have put out a new song every other year for fun and continue to do the Momentous Music Fest each year to benefit different charities we care about. Over the past 10 years, we have raised over $200,000 to benefit 10 nonprofit organizations.

When I pull into my driveway in my 2025 Toyota First Edition Landcruiser in underground gray, three cars sit in our four-car garage: a black four-door Jeep Wrangler for my son Jace, a white Honda Pilot for EmmyLu, and a gray 2035 Tesla Model X for the family.

As I get out of my car, my kids are waiting in the living room with their backpacks and camping supplies, ready for our next adventure. Our goal is to explore all 50 states by going on two-yearly trips to top glamping destinations in the US.

Pictures of my family and all the experiences and places we have traveled line the walls of our six-bedroom home, including photos from our African Safari, the Great Wall of China, Bali, Singapore, Fiji, Australia, ski trips to Breckinridge, Anguilla, Rome, Machu Picchu, Southern France, and Sutherland Falls in New Zealand. At our family dinners, we often talk about all the memories and experiences we had on these trips and talk and dream about the places we will go in the future.

As I sit in my favorite leather chair near the fireplace in our living room, and look out our grand windows, I hear the kids having conversations in our hot tub with their friends. I can smell the scent of fresh-cut grass and flowers coming in from the screen door of our sunroom and can feel the warmth of the sun on my face as I prepare a speech for an upcoming speaking event.

On Saturdays, we have a movie night in our backyard with all the neighbors and good friends with our 25-foot outdoor movie screen. The kids make popcorn in our old-fashioned popcorn maker, cook gourmet smores over our fire pit, and play video games later in our game room on our classic arcade console.

I spend a lot of my time meeting with my top 50 clients, guiding them in reaching their dreams and aspirations, and delivering advice that creates financial peace of mind and a richer life.

I have a modern and beautiful office in Woodbury with hardwood floors, a brushed steel logo of Momentous Wealth Advisors in the lobby, built-in bookshelves with hard copy books I've read, a fireplace with four elegant leather chairs in the lobby, an exposed brick wall, a collection of meaningful art, and a large framed map with pictures of clients and the places they have been.

Every month, we look forward to attending two or three live concerts by all our favorite artists. Our goal is to always be near the front row and sing loud to our favorite songs. We also always try to catch a comedy show when the best comedians come to town.

I only take on five new client relationships yearly, and every client values my counsel and advice. As I file my taxes in 2034, an unbelievable sense of accomplishment and humbleness for the obstacles I fought through, limiting beliefs I squashed, and the life we now enjoy comes over me. I truly M.A.D.E. something of the last 10 years and have put our family on a path of living a fully engaged and charged life full of experiences and freedom.

The Wealth Decisions Podcast is in its 500th episode, has been listened to by over one million people, and has made an extraordinary difference in the lives of individuals worldwide.

Momentous Wealth Advisors has been featured on CNBC, Forbes, Yahoo Finance, and Bloomberg Business.

The Momentous Wealth Open Pickleball Tournament has grown to over 500 participants and has become the largest tournament in the Midwest. It has attracted the top touring pros in the United States.

We spend four to six weeks each year at our villa in Anguilla on Meads Bay. While we are there, we spend a lot of time at our favorite restaurants and beach shacks, which include Blanchard's, The Sunshine Shack, and The Dune Preserve. I can hear the reggae music bouncing off the palm trees and feel the silky white sand massaging my toes as we sit on our beach chairs near our three-bedroom villa. I have my uke in hand to practice for an upcoming acoustic show at the Sunshine Shack and The Dune Preserve, where I sing songs I have written about my travels in the Caribbean and old Brian David Band songs.

We also spend a lot of time in the summer in Minnesota on the St. Croix River in our Chaparral Cruiser boat, which we dock at the Marina in downtown Afton. We meet up with good friends, stop at riverside restaurants, and tell stories of our travels and adventures.

We have been fortunate enough to give back and last year gave $20k to CrossRoads Church, $20k to the Park Nicollet Growing Through Grief Program, and $20k to the Red Cross. We get invited each year to the Red Cross Large Donor Gala Dinner and are doing mission trips with our church as a family, instilling the principles of giving back in our kids.

The book *Momentous Decisions: 7 Steps to Better Health, More Wealth, and a Richer Life* has sold 250,000 copies worldwide and allowed me to speak at special large events 10 times a year.

When I go to bed at night, I sleep soundly, knowing that I helped make an extraordinary difference in the lives of my family, friends, clients, and people wanting to live a richer life filled with more meaning, accomplishment, difference, and experiences. I feel so grateful for my life and look forward to the next decade filled with more amazing experiences and adventures.

Summary of Developing a MOMENTOUS 10-Year Vision

Creating a vision for your life will create a pull in you from the future, rather than having to push yourself each day. It will compel you, ignite you, give you a stronger reason to get up each day to fulfill your long-term goals and help you be on a path to living a richer life. The next step is to make a plan to fulfill your long-term vision. A plan that takes into account all the things that are important to you. A plan to be better. A plan to build and keep more of your wealth. A plan to be healthy, happy, and more fulfilled.

MOMENTOUS DECLARATION #12

I understand that what I focus on expands. I have a vivid compelling vision I want for my life, wealth, and health.

STEP 5:   Make a Life, Wealth, and Health Plan.

As Jim Rohn said, "Without a future well-defined, we take hesitant steps." Five or 10 years from now, do you want to be where you are? Do you want to be thinking the same things? Do you want to say I am glad I did, or I wished I would have?

Life A.

Visualize for a moment: 10 years from now, you will be financially independent, physically fit, healthy, and living this richer life you have wanted. If you had enough money to meet your needs, wants, and wishes and had your energy and vitality back, how would you be living your life? How would you feel? What would be different for you and your family?

Life B.

Now I want you to visualize for a moment 10 years from now, you are financially secure, but your health is poor, and you are feeling unfulfilled and lacking purpose. Even though you have enough money to meet your needs and some of your wants, you can't do all the things you want to do. How would you feel? What do you wish you could feel? What would you want to be different? What would you change? Do you have any regrets?

Most people would want to feel the way that the person in life A is feeling. We deserve a richer life, and we can achieve it, but only if we have a plan.

Designing a richer life can be as simple as bringing back into your life things you were once passionate about. Think back for a minute. What did you want your life to look like? Is it what you thought life could and should be? Is it the life you envisioned when you were younger?

Think back for a moment to when you were a younger. What were you passionate about? Write down the top three things that you remember being passionate about:

1. _____
2. _____
3. _____

I was passionate about art, music, and freestyle trick riding. I loved to draw black and white pencil pictures of people. I loved writing songs and attempting to sing (I didn't find my voice until I was in my late 20s). From the age of nine to about the age of 13, I was an amateur Flatland Freestyle BMX trick rider (I could link a funky chicken to a spastic freak squeak like no other). I haven't drawn since high school. I still write music, but the last time I pulled my old GT trick bike out, I landed flat on my back. Some things will always be in your life, and others will never be in your life again (freestyle trick riding being one of them for me). But why can't I bring art back into my life more? Some psychologists prescribe to patients that they bring an old passion back into their lives to bring more joy and happiness. If you're not happy, think back to the things that used to bring you joy and happiness. Find one and start doing it again. Today.

Now, think back to when you were young. Write down three things you wanted for your life: what you wanted to do, what you wanted to be, and what you envisioned for your life:

1. _____
2. _____
3. _____

I wanted to travel the world as much as possible. Ever since my speech class in high school, I have wanted to be a public speaker. I envisioned a life of health, wealth, and fulfillment. Today, I have traveled the world and have many more places to go. I feel like I am in the best shape of my life. I have done some public speaking, but I know I want to do more of that in the future. I am building my wealth to have financial freedom one day. I am fulfilled, but only when I do things that make a difference in people's lives.

That is why I designed a framework for living a richer life. The M.A.D.E. LifePlan is about being intentional about creating a life going forward that will bring you closer to living that life you once envisioned but lost sight of or to live a completely different life than you have been used to living. Many of the things you learned in the life, wealth, and health decisions chapters will be a guide to creating a M.A.D.E. LifePlan that centers around what is most important to you right now that is in line with the new standards you want for your life, health, and wealth over time. A better life needs a plan.

Your M.A.D.E. Life, Wealth, and Health Plan

Your road map to create the life you deserve is the M.A.D.E. LifePlan.

It will take time and require thought and reflection, but when you are done, it will be yours and yours alone. You will be able to look at it and say: This is who I am. This is what I stand for. This is what is important to me.

The M.A.D.E. LifePlan is your framework to create a vision for how your life will be and can be. You can look back at your life and say, I really made something of it.

The acronym M.A.D.E. stands for:

M – Meaning

A – Accomplish

D – Difference

E – Experiences

When you do a Google search to find your purpose, how many results come up? Last I checked, about 173 million. People want more meaning in their lives. They want to stand for something. They want to know their purpose. What your purpose is can be easier to find than you think. Dr. Wayne Dyer certainly thought it was. Dr. Dyer said, "A sense of purpose isn't something that you find, it's something you are." I believe our purpose is simply to be our best selves, find meaning in life's simple things, accomplish things that are important to us, make a difference in the lives of others, and create memorable experiences that bring life zest and joy.

MEANING

When it comes to meaning there are eight areas of your life that can add more meaning and balance. Those are part of what I call the LifePlan. And yes, it is in the form of another acronym.

L.I.F.E.P.L.A.N.

L – Love/Family – How strong your family is and how deep your love is with the ones you care about.

I – Interests/Hobbies – Hobbies, interests, and passions bring joy to your life.

F – Faith/Spirituality – How strong your faith is and how connected you are to something greater.

E – Emotional Health – How healthy you are emotionally leads to lower stress, a better outlook, and gives you more energy to live a better life.

P – Personal Growth – How committed you are to growth adds a positivity to your life and allows you to handle better what life throws your way.

L – Life Fulfillment – How fulfilled you feel creates purpose and peace of mind.

A – Appreciation/Gratitude – Creates a feeling of gratefulness for what you have.

N – Needs of Others/Generosity – Adds a feeling of worth and helpfulness.

Ask yourself, "What three areas do I need or want to improve now on my LifePlan to have better balance and more meaning?" Rank how you feel right now about each area of life that gives you more meaning on a scale of 1 to 10. The areas you score the lowest on may be what you want to focus on first over the next 90 days.

L – Love and family 1 2 3 4 5 6 7 8 9 10
I – Interests/Hobbies 1 2 3 4 5 6 7 8 9 10
F – Faith/Spirituality 1 2 3 4 5 6 7 8 9 10
E – Emotional Health 1 2 3 4 5 6 7 8 9 10
P – Personal Growth 1 2 3 4 5 6 7 8 9 10
L – Life Fulfillment 1 2 3 4 5 6 7 8 9 10
A – Appreciation/Gratitude 1 2 3 4 5 6 7 8 9 10
N – Needs of Others/Generosity 1 2 3 4 5 6 7 8 9 10

What areas could you improve to bring more balance into your life? Because we live in a world that has become values-less and is often in direct conflict with the things that matter most, it will be hard to live this balanced life. It won't be easy to live this lifestyle because everywhere we go, someone or some company is saying that whatever we have isn't good enough. I am here to tell you that if it is good enough for you, it is good enough. If it meets your new standards, then it is good enough. If it makes you feel more fulfilled, then it is good enough. If it gives you more meaning and keeps you on a path to a richer life, then it is good enough.

To live a richer life, you need to have balance. Most of the time, we spend more energy on planning our next vacation than we do on our own lives, which is a pretty important thing to do since you only have one. Most people move into a lazy pattern of letting life happen. I have been guilty of this many times in my life. I believe we are all here to live our own stories – one that is unique, one that is authentic. We don't have to let life just happen.

While money and wealth are very important, I believe that if one lives a life that is balanced and growing in all the areas of your M.A.D.E. LifePlan, they will be rich with life. I believe that money should not be pursued, but it will be attracted to you by the person you become. So, commit to improve. Start with the areas that would make the short term the best it can be, so that your feelings of the immediate future are charged with life. Evaluating your life balance will show where the priorities of improvement need to be. Your goal is to improve in three areas every 90 days in the meaning category of your M.A.D.E. LifePlan. You will most likely never score a perfect 10 in every area of your life, but the idea is to understand what areas you want to improve to create an intentional plan to create more meaning and live a richer life.

So, what three areas of your life are most important for you to improve right now to make this the best year ever? Love/Family? Emotional Health? Faith/Spirituality?

Once you decide the areas you want to focus on to bring your life more meaning, you will want to start thinking about the things you can do to improve those areas. For instance, if emotional health is very important to you right now, brainstorm all the things you could do to improve your emotional health.

Things you could do for your emotional health:

1. Develop a mindfulness practice.
2. Reach out to a good friend.
3. Establish boundaries at work or at home.
4. Journal each day.
5. Get out in nature.
6. Do something active.
7. Get eight hours of sleep per night.
8. Set some goals.
9. Work on your self-talk.
10. Seek professional support like therapy.

After you have listed at least 10 things, circle the one that could make the most impact over the next 90 days. That is the one that you will focus on in your M.A.D.E. 90-Day Action Plan in that LifePlan category.

If improving love and family are really important to you right now, list out all the things you could do to improve your most important relationships.

Things you could do to improve your most important relationships:

1. Get better at listening.
2. Be more present each day.
3. Express feelings better.
4. Communicate honestly.
5. Show appreciation each day.
6. Spend more quality time.
7. Apologize or forgive someone.
8. Do small acts of kindness.
9. Follow through with things you said you would do.
10. Develop life goals with your family.

These are just some of the things you could do to improve your most important relationships. After you have listed at least 10 things, circle the one that could make the most impact over the next 90 days. That is the one that you will focus on in your M.A.D.E. 90-Day Action Plan.

ACCOMPLISH

It is time to get clear on what you want to accomplish with your health and wealth. When it comes to what you want to ACCOMPLISH, what is your ideal financial situation? What is your ideal level of health?

Your ideal financial situation:

Example. My ideal financial situation would be:

1. To have $50k in a money-market account for emergencies.
2. To put away 20% of my income per month.
3. To have $100k in a taxable investment account.
4. To have a financial plan and be on the right path to retire at age 62.

5. To be able to help my kids pay for half of their college expenses.
6. To be able to give $10k per year to the causes I care about.
7. To have a net worth of $1 million by the time I am 50.

Your ideal level of health:

Example. My ideal level of health would be:

1. To lose two inches off my waist.
2. To be active every day.
3. To lower my cholesterol and blood pressure.
4. To be able to play pickleball three days a week without feeling sore.
5. To be flexible and be able to touch my toes again.
6. To be able to do 30 push ups.
7. To feel strong and confident.
8. To have more energy.

In the M.A.D.E. Life Action Plan you are going to focus on ONE MOMENTOUS THING you can do every day, every week, or every month to accomplish your most important health and wealth goals which I will give you a framework for to develop in your 90-Day plan.

DIFFERENCE

Plan out what you are going to do every 90 days to make a difference in the lives of those you care about or the causes most important to you. These can be little things or big things. It is about being intentional and thoughtful. Here are some actionable things you could do to make a difference in the lives of your kids, your relationship with your spouse or partner, your friends, and causes:

For your kids:

- Start "special time" traditions like Sunday morning pancake-making with each child individually.

- Share your day's highs and lows at dinner every day.
- Write them small notes of encouragement to find in their lunch boxes or post them on the mirror in their bathroom.
- Talk through their problems without jumping to solutions.
- Support their interests even if they differ from yours.
- Help them set goals and celebrate their wins, not just the outcome.
- Involve them in meal planning, grocery shopping, and cooking.
- Teach practical skills like doing laundry, repairing things, and money management.
- Teach them how to set boundaries.
- Model healthy habits.
- Create screen-free zones and times for time to connect.
- Volunteer for things as a family.
- Talk about different viewpoints and cultures.

For your spouse or partner:

- Remember and acknowledge important dates beyond the obvious ones.
- Show appreciation for things they do.
- Create space for them to pursue their passions.
- Plan date nights to do things you both enjoy.
- Learn their love language and show affection in ways meaningful to them.
- Share dreams and set joint goals for your future.
- Make financial decisions together.
- Take over some of their to-dos when they're stressed.
- Send unexpected thoughtful messages during the day.
- Notice and comment on positive changes they make.
- Pay attention to things they share and follow up later.

For friends:

- Set reminders for important dates and events in their lives.
- Offer to help rather than "let me know if you need anything."
- Check in regularly, not just during tough times.
- Create traditions like monthly game nights or morning coffee.
- Remember details about their family members and ask about them – be honest and compassionate when they need feedback.
- Be a growth friend and support their growth.
- Create a care package during tough times.
- Remember the things they like.
- Connect them with people in your network that may be able to help them or their business.
- Share things you have learned that you think could help them.

For causes:

- Join a mutual aid network in your community that helps neighbors with food, housing, childcare, or other essential needs.
- Set up recurring monthly donations to your church or a cause you are passionate about.
- Volunteer your professional skills pro bono to a nonprofit.
- Start conversations with friends and family about important issues you would like to try to help with.
- Get involved in city council meetings or advisory boards.
- Make lifestyle changes to impact the environment like minimizing single-use plastics or reducing meat consumption.
- Start or join a workplace giving circle where you all pool donations to support local causes.
- Support local business that align with your values like worker-owned cooperatives, B corporations, or companies with strong environmental practices.

The key to making a difference is consistency and authenticity. It's about finding meaningful ways to show up for the people in your life. Start with One Momentous Thing you can do to make the biggest difference and soon they will become habits. I get it, we are all busy. Sometimes we are so busy that we forget how important our connections are and how much we need them. Making a difference in the lives of the people most important to us will make life feel richer. It will not only make others feel good, it will make you feel good.

Your Making a Difference Life Vision

When it comes to what DIFFERENCE you want to make, ask yourself what the most important future contributions you want to make are. The framework would be:

I gave …

I made …

I impacted …

I left …

EXAMPLE OF YOUR LONG-TERM VISION OF MAKING A DIFFERENCE

My most important future CONTRIBUTIONS will be that:

I GAVE my family opportunities that most don't have in life. A life of abundance, opportunity, and privilege.

I MADE A DIFFERENCE to the causes we care about, including our church, the Red Cross, The Rotary International Foundation, and the Animal Humane Society.

I IMPACTED others in a way that changed the direction of their lives, both personally and professionally. I made a difference by motivating and inspiring others to do more and be more.

I LEFT a legacy of life lessons for my kids, principles to guide them, and an abundance of wealth that will allow my family to be taken care of and proud of the work I have accomplished in my lifetime.

In your M.A.D.E. 90-Day Life Action Plan you are going to work on ONE MOMENTOUS THING you could to do make a daily difference in the lives of your family, your friends, and the causes you care about.

E – Experiences

Life is all about the moments and experiences you have. The ones you tell stories about for years to come. The ones that remain in our hearts and minds our whole life. Plan out your experiences for the next 90 days so you have things to look forward to. Think about all the things you could do to create experiences for your family and friends. Look at events coming up, trips on your experience list, and brainstorm ideas to create experiences you could have with your family. When it comes to planning things with our family or friends, this is probably the easiest thing to do in your M.A.D.E. LifePlan because it is something we have done our whole life. We have planned vacations, trips, concerts, etc., but if you are like me, if I am not intentional and make an effort about planning things, especially with friends, a whole year goes by, and I haven't spent any quality time with my closest friends. It is much easier to plan things like trips with your family, but it is a little harder to be more intentional about creating simple things you can do each week to create lasting memories. In the life decisions chapter I listed out some experiences you could do with your family in the first life decision, "experience more things." Create your list of experiences and maybe even have a designated day that you do them. Like Adventure Sundays, where each family member takes turns planning a small adventure. Learn to make pasta from scratch. Go geocaching. Go to a new hiking spot at a local state park. Take a road trip. Draw together. Take a painting class. Start a family garden together. Have weekly sunset picnics at different locations. Do some apple picking and making cider from scratch. Have a "Mystery Day" where one person plans a complete surprise day for the family. Create a home "restaurant" where kids help plan the menu, decorate, and serve as waiters. Have a backyard camping night. Buy a dart board and have a family cricket tournament.

Get the next trip booked you want to experience, whether that is with your family or good friends. Plan out some of the fun things you are going to do when you are there, but leave some room for spontaneity.

Make out your own experience list and start adding some of them into your life every 90 days. Make some of them rituals. Your life will feel richer just knowing you have some things planned to look forward to and those memorable fun experiences will become part of your life that you and your family will remember for years to come.

STEP 6:   SHARE Your Plan with Someone.

One of the keys to positive change is to share your goals with someone. Write that goal down and share it with someone important to you. There was a *USA Today* study done that said that people who think about a goal, write it down, and share it with someone have an 80% chance of reaching that goal. The study also showed that people with goals just thought about and not written down or shared only have a 10% chance of reaching their goals. Write your map. Plot your destination. When you get there you'll know you made it, because you had an end goal in mind. Make sure they are someone who will be there to support you every step of the way, and hopefully, they are all-in with you as well, creating their own plan.

STEP 7:   Work on ONE MOMENTOUS THING in Each Part of Your M.A.D.E. LifePlan every 90 Days.

Looking out five years or even 10 years is daunting. The best way to reach goals is to have a long-term vision but a short-term plan. Breaking things down into 90-day increments is the most effective way to do this.

To get started on living a more balanced and fulfilled life, it can be overwhelming to do all the things you need to do. We know what being overwhelmed can do: It creates inaction. It can paralyze us. That is why it is important to start small. I created what I call the M.A.D.E. 90-Day Life Action Plan. It involves starting with ONE MOMENTOUS THING you can do to improve in each area of your life. A momentous thing is a decision of significant importance, especially of its bearing on the future. It is something that can have the greatest impact in the short term but also when done over time will help you live a richer life with more meaning and balance, make a bigger difference to the people and causes you care about, accomplish your most important goals, and create and plan of experiences to look forward to.

The M.A.D.E. 90-Day Life Action Plan

M – MEANING

What three areas do I need or want to improve on my LifePlan to have better balance over the next 90 days?

- **L** – Love and family
- **I** – Interests/Hobbies
- **F** – Faith/Spirituality
- **E** – Emotional Health

P – Personal Growth

L – Life Fulfillment

A – Appreciation/Gratitude

N – Needs of Others/Generosity

List the three things in your LifePlan you want to focus on over the next 90 days:

1. _____

2. _____

3. _____

One of the most important things when working on something in your life is to schedule the thing you are going to do. Put it on the calendar whether it is something you will do daily, weekly, or monthly. It is not just about listing what you will do, but writing down when you will do it.

What ONE MOMENTOUS THING can I do in each of the top three areas of my LifePlan to make the biggest impact over the next 90 days?

Area 1: _____

ONE MOMENTOUS THING: _____

Schedule it: Every day/week at: _____ a.m./p.m.

Area 2:_____

ONE MOMENTOUS THING: _____

Schedule it: Every day/week at: _____ a.m./p.m.

Area 3: _____

ONE MOMENTOUS THING: _____

Schedule it: Every day/week at: _____ a.m./p.m.

A – ACCOMPLISH

What is the ONE MOMENTOUS THING you could do to ACCOMPLISH your desired level of success over the next 90 days?

1. _____

Schedule it: Every day at: _____ a.m./p.m.

What is the ONE MOMENTOUS THING you could do to ACCOMPLISH your desired level of health over the next 90 days?

1. _____

Schedule it: Every day at: _____ a.m./p.m.

What is the ONE MOMENTOUS THING you could do to ACCOMPLISH your desired level of wealth over the next 90 days?

1. _____

Schedule it: Every month on the _____

D – DIFFERENCE

What is the ONE MOMENTOUS THING you could do to make a difference in the lives of your family, your friends, and the causes you care about over the next 90 days?

FAMILY _____

Schedule it: _____/ _____/_____

FRIENDS _____

Schedule it: _____/ _____/_____

CAUSES _____

Schedule it: _____/ _____/_____

E – EXPERIENCES

What is the ONE MOMENTOUS THING you could do to create experiences and memorable moments with your family and friends? What is the one trip you want to experience in the next 90 Days?

FAMILY _____

Schedule it: Every week on _____ at _____ a.m./p.m.

FRIENDS _____

Schedule it: Every week on _____ at _____ a.m./p.m.

TRIPS

_____ Schedule it _____/_____/_____

_____ Schedule it _____/_____/_____

_____ Schedule it _____/_____/_____

EVENTS (Live music, comedy, etc.)

_____ Schedule it _____/_____/_____

_____ Schedule it _____/_____/_____

_____ Schedule it _____/_____/_____

_____ Schedule it _____/_____/_____

_____ Schedule it _____/_____/_____

_____ Schedule it _____/_____/_____

Here is an example of a M.A.D.E. Life 90-Day Action Plan

MEANING

What three areas do I need or want to improve now on my LifePlan to have better balance?

1. Family/Love
2. Faith
3. Appreciation/Gratitude

What ONE MOMENTOUS THING can I do in each of the top three areas of my LifePlan to make the biggest impact over the next 90 days?

Area 1: Love/Family

ONE MOMENTOUS THING
Be present and engaged every day and practice the three As.
Schedule it: Every day before dinner at 4:30 p.m.

Area 2: Faith

ONE MOMENTOUS THING
Pray with my kids.
Schedule it: Every night at 9 p.m.

Area 3: Appreciation/Gratitude

ONE MOMENTOUS THING
Journal every day what I am grateful for.
Schedule it: Every day at 5:30 a.m.

ACCOMPLISH

What is the ONE MOMENTOUS THING you could do to get closer to ACCOMPLISHING your desired level of health over the next 90 days?

Work out or do something active every day first thing in the morning.

Schedule it: Every morning at 7 a.m.

What is the ONE MOMENTOUS THING you could do to get closer to ACCOMPLISHING your desired level of wealth over the next 90 days?

Pay myself first at least 20% of my income and invest that for the future in my Roth 401k, Roth IRA, and a taxable account.

Schedule it: Every month on the 3rd.

What is the ONE MOMENTOUS THING you could do to ACCOMPLISH your desired level of success over the next 90 days?

Time-block every day.

Schedule it: Every day from 8 to 10 a.m.

DIFFERENCE

What is the ONE MOMENTOUS THING you could to do make a daily DIFFERENCE in the lives of your family, your friends, your clients, and the causes you care about over the next 90 days?

Family: Talk about our roses and thorns for the day.

Schedule it: Every night during dinner.

Friends: Call a friend and tell them how much I appreciate our friendship.

Schedule it: Every Friday at 3 p.m.

Causes: Sign up for a meal packing event through church to help families in need.

Schedule it: 15 March 2025.

EXPERIENCES

What is the ONE MOMENTOUS THING you could do to create EXPERIENCES and memorable moments with your family and friends over the next 90 days? What one trip do you want to experience?

Family: Play cards or games as a family.

Schedule it: Every Thursday night after dinner.

Friends: Get a big group of friends to go to a concert together.

Schedule it: Snow Patrol on 29 March 2025.

Trips:

Go on a ski trip to Keystone, Colorado. Schedule it: 20 February 2025.

Go on Spring Break to Turks and Caicos. Schedule it: 10 March 2025.

Events:

Nick Swardson comedy show. Schedule it: 1 October 2025.

Shane Gillis comedy show. Schedule it: 22 February 2025.

Drew Holcomb music show. Schedule it: 2 March 2025.

When you start with ONE MOMENTOUS THING you can do, you will start making visible progress in each area of your life. You will start to build more balance, which will allow you to take steps toward living a richer life. There are going to be good days, not so good days, and perfect days. Don't let a not so perfect day derail you or discourage you. Living a richer life is not about perfect. It is about having an intentional plan to make progress in all the things that are important to you right now and work toward your vision on how you want your life to be. Enjoy the process of becoming better. Feel good about having a plan to build your wealth, become healthier, and live a life with more meaning, accomplishment, difference, and experiences.

Every 90 days you may choose to continue doing some of the same things, or bring other things into the mix of your M.A.D.E. Life Action Plan. You might choose to work on three entirely different things in the meaning category of your plan. Your experiences may be the thing that changes the most, because those are the things that will bring you the most joy and excitement into your life. The last two weeks of your 90-day plan is when you decide what you want to focus on and plan for your next 90-Day M.A.D.E. LifePlan. The idea is that over the course of the year, you will ingrain new things into your daily routine to bring more meaning into your life. You will have created new standards and habits to accomplish what is most important to you. You will have focused more on making a difference. You will have planned out your experiences to give you things to look forward to. Over one year, you will be better. You will be in the process of becoming healthier. You will have a plan to build and keep more of your wealth. Your relationships will be better. Your life will feel richer.

To get a complimentary M.A.D.E. Life Action Plan, go to: https:// momentouswealthadvisors.com/madelifeplan.

Living a Momentous Life

To live a richer life, we need to change our thoughts on what is possible for us, make new standards, and create a better vision for what our lives can be. Our past has nothing to do with our future. What we focus on each day expands. Good or bad. Fixate on positivity, and it builds and creates more happiness and positivity. When you're happier, you're better. When you're better, you'll have more of everything you deserve. More happiness. More success. More love. More fulfillment. More purpose. More meaning.

We are here in this life right now to live a unique, authentic life to the fullest. I believe that we have an obligation to be the best self we can be each day. To make a difference in the lives of the people most important to us. To be our best selves, we need to be intentional and committed to lifelong growth and balance in our lives. Many things can change our lives, but only a handful can truly make all the difference. That is what this journey is all about – finding the things that will make a difference in your life and those you care about. My reason for this book was for you to have a place to find them. Not everything is going to resonate with you now, but I hope that you will find the things that will make a difference to you. So that a year from now, three years from now, or 10 years from now you will have lived a life closer to exceptional. A life that feels richer.

What are the things you have forgotten about what you wanted for your life? What has gotten in the way? Well, for most of us, life has gotten in the way. Responsibilities, bills, etc. Why should something we were once passionate about be left on the back burner? Sometimes, we wonder why we are not fulfilled in the present moment but forget the things that brought happiness and fulfillment in the first place. Bring back something into your life today, that you were once passionate about. If it was a sport, join a league. If it was a talent or hobby, get what you need to start that hobby again. If it was something you were really good at, find a way to be good at it again and incorporate it back into your life somewhere.

I'm sure you've heard that the most common things said by folks who are on their death bed is regret – regret not over the bad things that they did, but more likely regret over the good things, the brave or risky things, that they didn't do. Don't let regret for the things you didn't do be on your mind on the day you pass.

This is your framework for living a richer life. Your framework to find and create more meaning, accomplishment, difference, and experiences in your life.

People who want to live richer lives create it, while people who don't just let life happen. Don't let life just happen. Create the life you want with the end in mind, and have fun along the way. Don't stress out about things you can't control. Be grateful for what you've done, but be inspired to do more, be more, and live more.

Get Started and Keeping Going

1. If you want to guarantee better results over a sustained period of time, the best approach is to make it easy to get started and create an environment that helps you keep going.
2. Focus on ONE MOMENTOUS THING you can do to make the biggest impact with your wealth habits, your health habits, or

something in your life, so your inner resistance doesn't start kicking in and you get too overwhelmed.

3. Be careful not to demand too much of yourself to early, or beat yourself up too often.

4. Make a story that empowers you rather than the one that has been holding you back.

5. When you are able to define your why behind your why, your actions will be more automatic without feeling stressed because you will be focusing on something that is internal and so important to you that you create a pull from the future.

6. Refer to your long-term vision often. Read it. Record and listen to it. If it doesn't excite you anymore, rewrite it.

Life, Health, Wealth Plan Advice Over Your First Year

Take a look at your environment. Is it conducive to reaching each one of your goals? People succeed long-term because their environment makes long-term success easier.

A. Health – Are you working out first thing in the morning before your willpower fades? Do something first thing, whether it is planks, a 10-minute H.I.I.T. Training Session, or a 20-minute walk. Get in the habit of doing something physical every day. Put your workout clothes next to your bed in the morning. Get an accountability partner. Join a gym that has coaches to inspire you and guide you.

B. Nutrition – Have you placed healthy foods at eye level and eliminated unhealthy snacks from your pantry? Your eyes will focus on things at eye level, so you will be more apt to choose healthy things. Have you signed up for a meal service or committed to doing some meal planning? Have you ordered some supplements and kept them visible on your counter so that you take them each day?

Did you order a 24 oz water bottle to make sure you drink enough water each day?

C. Wealth – Have you set up a separate account to funnel money into that is not easily accessible to make sure you don't spend sporadically on things you don't need? Have you found a way to live below your means? Have you decided the amount you are going to pay yourself first and set up an automatic investment program? Have you set goals for where you want to be financially three years from now? Five years from now? Ten years from now?

D. Life – Have you committed to bringing the three As into your most important relationships? Have you bought a positive book on mindset? Have you practiced gratitude? Have you been more intentional about creating joy in your life?

SUMMARY

As Jim Rohn said, "The worst thing one can do is not to try, to be aware of what one wants and not give in to it, to spend years in silent hurt wondering if something could have materialized—never knowing."

Transformation doesn't happen overnight. It doesn't happen in an instant. It comes from a plan to live a richer life. It comes from a commitment to improvement and a determination and desire to make those improvements new standards in your life. Start telling yourself "you deserve it," and then start deserving it by taking action. Start making some new agreements with yourself. Make an agreement with yourself to always bring your best self to every situation. Make an agreement to be of value to those you care about, to your friends, and to the world. Make an agreement to yourself to be more present and engaged in your life. Make an agreement to always find ways to go the extra mile in everything you do. Make an agreement with yourself to stop telling the story you have always told yourself. Make an agreement to be better than you were yesterday. Make an agreement to take action and live with intention.

Like Dr. Wayne Dyer said, "Sense of purpose isn't something that you find, it's something that you are." I don't think we have one and only one purpose and I think you will drive yourself crazy trying to find your one and only purpose. I think we have many things that can be our purpose. If you believe Dr. Wayne Dyer, your purpose is who you are. Who you are to those you care about. Who you are to your friends. Who you are to complete strangers. Our purpose is really simple when you think of it that way. Our purpose is to be our best selves and bring value to those most important to us. Our purpose is to bring more meaning to our lives by being intentional. Our purpose is to accomplish our most important goals without sacrificing our most important relationships. Our purpose is to make a difference no matter how small or big. Our purpose is to create experiences in our lives that give life zest and stories to tell that make us smile.

When you live a life by design, you will be different. Your success will be different. Your level of wealth will be different. Your relationships will be different. Your life will be different. Different in a way only you will be able to describe when you get there. You will be a difference maker in the lives of your family, your friends, and the causes you care about. You will be living this richer life you have always hoped for. Enjoy the journey and celebrate your wins. Focus on the process, not just the end result. You will feel proud having a plan, whether you have good or bad days, because you know you are on a new path to live a better life.

Your past is the only thing in your way right now. Your past beliefs. Your past circumstances. Your past does not define you and doesn't have to control the direction of your life. We can be defined, or we can be reminded of who we are and what we are capable of. I hope this book has given you some ideas and tools to help you live a better life. A more fulfilling life. A life by design never to be defined again.

The past is done. All that matters is what you are going to do right now to make things better. Each day is an opportunity to make progress on your vision or tread water. Choose progress. Start designing how you want your life to be going forward. I hope that 10 years from now, you will be so glad you read this book and took action toward living a richer life.

In his book *Life's Greatest Lesson*, Allen Hunt tells the story of Grandma Lavish, who lived an extraordinary life and had people lined up at her funeral service, and no one wanted to leave the cemetery. The story is told through the eyes of her grandson, Christopher. He asked his grandpa the question, "Grandpa, why do you think no one wanted to leave the cemetery? Why wouldn't they go home?" His Grandfather took a deep breath and said, "Your grandmother was special, Christopher. She was a giver. And people loved her for that. I don't think she ever really knew how many people she had touched. She never realized how much people loved her. She just loved to give." She wore a bright orange rubber bracelet with the letters L.E.G.S. in black on it. It was an acronym for how she lived her life and advice we could all live by.

The letters stood for:

L: Love all you can

E: Earn all you can

G: Give all you can

S: Save all you can

This is what she believed in. This is what she stood for.

So, the big question we have asked before in this book, but let's ask it one last time: What will you have stood for? What will people remember? What will you have M.A.D.E. of your life?

APPENDIX 1

MOMENTOUS DECLARATIONS

MOMENTOUS DECLARATION #1

I will make health my priority because I want to live a long, active life filled with experiences and enjoy the wealth I create.

MOMENTOUS DECLARATION #2

My past has nothing to do with the future I can create for myself and my family.

MOMENTOUS DECLARATION #3

My beliefs are nothing more than a thought I have kept thinking and I can change my thoughts, therefore I can change my beliefs.

MOMENTOUS DECLARATION #4

Money has no emotions. It does not have energy. Humans do, therefore I can change the emotions and energy I have around money.

MOMENTOUS DECLARATION #5

I am focused on designing a richer life rather than just making a living.

MOMENTOUS DECLARATION #6

I believe I am capable of living a richer life. The amount of my success in life is determined by the amount of my belief.

MOMENTOUS DECLARATION #7

I am committed to personal growth because my wealth and success will only grow to the extent that I grow.

MOMENTOUS DECLARATION #8

Instead of thinking about how much money I don't have, I will think about how much money I will have in the future with my plan for financial independence or freedom.

MOMENTOUS DECLARATION #9

I keep all my reasons close because they are the foundation of positive feelings that lead to more action and better results.

MOMENTOUS DECLARATION #10

I will focus on opportunities, not obstacles, because I have goals I "must" achieve.

MOMENTOUS DECLARATION #11

I am committed to changing my current situation for my wealth and health by setting new standards for myself personally and professionally.

MOMENTOUS DECLARATION #12

I understand that what I focus on expands. I have a vivid compelling vision I want for my life, wealth, and health.

APPENDIX 2

RICHER LIFE MAINTENANCE

When you lose your focus. Read or rewrite your REASONS.

When you've gotten pessimistic. Read a POSITIVE BOOK.

When you've gotten too comfortable. Set new STANDARDS.

When you've lost faith in your potential. Read the DECLARATIONS.

When you've lost your drive. Write a new COMPELLING VISION.

When you've met your goals too easily. Set BIGGER GOALS.

When you've followed your plan, always REWARD yourself.

When your life lacks meaning, reassess your L.I.F.E.P.L.A.N.

APPENDIX 3

BOOKS THAT INSPIRED THIS BOOK

1. "Who Moved My Cheese" by Spencer Johnson
2. "7 Habits of Highly Effective People" by Stephen Covey
3. "The Last Lecture" by Randy Pausch
4. "The Secret" by Rhonda Byrne
5. "How to Win Friends and Influence People" by Dale Carnegie
6. "Think and Grow Rich" by Napoleon Hill
7. "Tuesdays with Morrie" by Mitch Albom
8. "Drive" by Daniel H. Pink
9. "Rich Dad, Poor Dad" by Robert Kiyosaki
10. "5 People You Meet in Heaven" by Mitch Albom
11. "Man's Search for Meaning" by Viktor Frankl
12. "The Power of Intention" by Dr. Wayne W. Dyer
13. "Secrets of a Millionaire Mind" by T. Harv Eker
14. "Law of Attraction" by Michael J Losier
15. "Attitude is Everything" by Keith Harrell
16. "Awaken the Giant Within" by Anthony Robbins
17. "The Charge" by Brendon Burchard
18. "Awakening to Your Life's Purpose" by Eckhart Tolle
19. "Make Today Count" by John C. Maxwell

20. "The Red Rubber Ball" by Kevin Carroll
21. "The Compound Effect" by Darren Hardy
22. "The 10X Rule" by Grant Cardone
23. "Goals" by Brian Tracey
24. "Drive From Within" by Michael Jordan
25. "The Motivation Manifesto" by Brendon Burchard
26. "The Power of Habit" by Charles Duhigg
27. "The Magic of Thinking Big" by David Schartz
28. "The 13 Secrets of World Class Achievers" by Vic Johnson
29. "The 12-Week Year" by Brian Moran
30. "What Got You Here Won't Get You There" by Marshall Goldsmith
31. "Change Your Thoughts, Change Your Life" by Dr. Wayne Dyer
32. "The Philosophy For Successful Living" by Jim Rohn
33. "Staying Up Up Up in a Down Down World" by Zig Ziglar
34. "The Richest Man in Babylon" by George Clason
35. "The Alchemist" by Paulo Coelho
36. "The Shift" by Dr. Wayne Dyer
37. "Switch" by Chip Health
38. "Learned Optimism" by Martin Seligman
39. "Best Year of Your Life" by Darren Hardy
40. "The 4-Hour Work Week" by Tim Ferris
41. "The Answer" by John Asseraf
42. "Law of Success" by Napoleon Hill
43. "Tested in the Trenches" by Ron Carson
44. "8 Best Success Lessons" by Jim Rohn
45. "The Million Dollar Financial Advisor" by David J. Mullen, Jr
46. "Supernova Advisor" by Robert D. Knapp
47. "Greatest Salesman in the World" by Og Mandino
48. "Miracle Morning" by Hal Elrod
49. "Power Questions to Win the Sale" by Andrew Sobel
50. "The Daily Edge" by David Horsager

51. "Selling with Emotional Intelligence" by Mitch Anthony
52. "The Language of Trust" by Michael Maslansky
53. "They Can't Eat You" by Marc Sparks
54. "The Practicing Mind" by Thomas Sterner
55. "Eat that Frog" by Brian Tracy
56. "Psychology of Winning in the 21st Century" by Dennis Waitley
57. "Gentle Art of Persuasion" by Tom Hopkins
58. "The One Thing" by Gary Keller
59. "The Story Factor" by Annette Simmons
60. "On the Back Burner" by Lee Storzinger
61. "Living Your Best Year Ever" by Darren Hardy
62. "Mindset Reset Process" by Rolf Magener
63. "Getting Everything You Can Out of What You Got" by Jay Abraham
64. "Triggers" by Marshall Goldsmith
65. "Law of Attraction" by Michael Hoiser
66. "The Slight Edge" by Jeff Olson
67. "Happiness Advantage" by Shawn Acher
68. "What Really Works – 7 F's" by Paul Batz
69. "The Art of Public Speaking" by Dale Carnegie
70. "Organize Tomorrow Today" by Jason Selk
71. "The Most Important Thing" by Howard Marks
72. "Executive Toughness" by Jason Selk
73. "The Four Agreements" by Don Miguel Ruiz
74. "Mindsight" by Daniel Siegel, MD
75. "Staying on the Path" by Dr. Wayne Dyer
76. "The Greatness Guide" by Robin Sharma
77. "Own Your Success" by Ben Newman
78. "The Sender" by Dr. Kevin Elko
79. "Kitchen Table Wisdom" by Rachel Naomi Remen
80. "Mindset – The New Psychology of Success" by Carol S. Dweck
81. "Thrive" by Arianna Huffington

82. "The Seven Spiritual Laws of Success" by Deepak Chopra
83. "The 15 Invaluable Laws of Growth" by John Maxwell
84. "Put Your Dream to the Test" by John Maxwell
85. "Beyond Willpower" by Alexander Loyd
86. "The Difference Maker" by John Maxwell
87. "The Willpower Instinct: How Willpower Works" by Kelly McGonigal, PhD
88. "A Message to Garcia" by Elbert Hubbard
89. "Charlie Munger" by Tren Griffen
90. "Emergence" by Derik Rydall
91. "Psychology of Selling" by Brian Tracy
92. "Irrationality" by Stuart Sutherland
93. "The Healing Codes" by Alexander Boyd
94. "E-cubed" by Pam Grout
95. "You Were Born Rich" by Bob Proctor
96. "Life's Greatest Lessons" by Hal Urban
97. "10 Powerful Phrases for Positive People" by Richard DeVos
98. "The Gift" by Shad Helmstetter
99. "The Road Less Traveled" by Dr. M. Scott Peck
100. "Unlimited" by Julian Micheals
101. "The Power of Neuroplasticity" by Shad Helmstetter
102. "The Winner's Bible" by Dr. Kerry Spackman
103. "The Big Leap" by Gay Hendricks
104. "Don't Believe Everything You Think" by Joseph Nguyen
105. "Rebel" by Graham Cochrane
106. "Experiencing the American Dream" by Mark Matson
107. "Breaking Free from Being Broke" by George Kamel
108. "Get Well, Stay Well" by Dr. Gemma Newman
109. "Feel Great, Lost Weight" by Dr. Rangan Chatterjee
110. "The Wealth Money Can't Buy" by Robin Sharma

111. "Happy Mind, Happy Life: The New Science of Mental Well-Being" by Dr. Rangan Chatterjee

112. "The Psychology of Wealth: Understanding Your Relationship with Money and Achieve Prosperity" by Charles Richards

113. "Everything is Figureoutable" by Marie Forleo

114. "The Greatness Mindset" by Lewis Howes

115. "How Are You, Really?" by Jenna Kutcher

116. "The Happiness Trap" by Russ Harris

117. "The Insight Cure" by John Sharp, MD

118. "Unleash the Power Within" by Tony Robbins

119. "Good Vibes" by Vex King

120. "Mojo" by Marshall Goldsmith

121. "The Purpose Driven Life" by Rich Warren and Morgan Huff

122. "Mission Possible" by Tim Tebow and A.J. Gregory

123. "The Power of Regret" by Daniel H. Pink

124. "When You're Ready, This is How You Heal" by Brianna Wiest

125. "The Happiness Advantage" by Shawn Achor

126. "Get Out of Your Own Way" by Dave Hollis

127. "Feeling Good" by David D. Burns, MD

128. "The High Five Habit" by Mel Robbins

129. "Atomic Habits" by James Clear

130. "Time and How to Spend It" by James Wallman

131. "Greenlights" by Matthew McConaughey

132. "Resilient" by Rich Hanson, PhD and Forrest Hanson

133. "Breaking the Habit of Being Yourself" by Dr. Joe Dispenza

APPENDIX 4

BRIAN DAVID SONGS 2009–2022

You can listen to Brian David Songs at: https://linktr.ee/briandavidband

"What Will Your Moment Be"?

CHORUS

What will your moment be
When will you start to see
Everything differently
What will your moment be?

VERSE 1

Grand thoughts compound, and time reveals…
Things you say out loud, will come when you believe
Life feels random, but your heart is constant
Waves come in tandem, to bring what you've wanted
What you've wanted, what you've wanted… so-oh-oh—

CHORUS

What will your moment be
When will you start to see
Everything differently
What will your moment be?

VERSE 2

We each have a story, inside our heads,
We keep a long vast inventory, we hang on to the threads
We strive for change, but we can't light the fire
It's not far out of range, if we find a real desire,
A real desire, a real desire—so-oh-oh

CHORUS

What will your moment be
When will you start to see
Everything differently
What will your moment be?

BRIDGE

Change your thoughts, change your life – change your mind, things go
right, it's not what you get, but who you become inside
See the stars all align, choose a life by design, stop waiting and wishing, it
will just come on by
It's not just going to come, not to everyone, unless you beat the drum,
unless you beat drum, unless you beat the drum
It's not just going to come, not to everyone, unless you beat the drum,
unless you beat drum, unless you beat the drum

RAP

It's not only possible, i thinks that its probable, you just need to believe, that nothing's impossible

Looking back at your chronicles and all of the obstacles, you got through them all, cuz success wasn't optional

Be sure you can have it all, know you're phenomenal, Don't go down the hole thinking only implausibles

Life can be volatile, but it can be optimal, if you dig down deep, you can find your true nautical

Nothing's affordable, if your goals are just nominal, you need bigger dreams, and you'll be nearly unstoppable

So trust that feeling deep in your abdominal, look in the mirror and say,

I AM possible, I AM possible, I AM POSSIBLE, I AM!

CHORUS

What will your moment be

When will you start to see

Everything differently

What will your moment be?

Feeling the moment, feeling the prize, feeling the fire deep down inside feeling the reasons, taking the call–feeling like your nearly ten feet tall

OUTRO

Find the why behind the why, before the music in you dies, find your moment right now

"Possible For You"

VERSE I

The new you wants to move ahead
But the old you hangs on to a thread
The new you wants to gets out of bed
But the old you stays too long in your head
We do it all the time
We are all only human and we soon find

CHORUS

There is something better looming on the other side
There is bigger starting deep down inside
There is that you no long—er can hide
It's the change you need
You just need to believe
That its not just possible but…possible…
For you… for you… for you——-

BRIDGE

So don't let sabotage… Turn you off
Don't let sabotage make you soft
Don't let sabotage keep you lost
So you don't change…you don't change

CHORUS

There is something better looming on the other side
There is bigger starting deep down inside
There is that you no long—er can hide
It's the change you need

You just need to believe
That it's not just possible but… possible…
For you… for you… for you

"What On Earth"

VERSE I

There's a pebble in your shoe, you know what to do
But you don't take it out, like all your doubts

PRE-CHORUS

Once you taste it… You'll never go back
So you don't waste it, slip through the cracks
Do you wonder, if there's more, more, more

CHORUS

What on earth…. are you on earth… for, are you on earth for
What on earth…. are you on earth… for, are you on earth for
What, now, why

VERSE II

Like a road never paved, a dream never craved
You go on without, not taking the route

PRE-CHORUS

Once you feel it there's more to come
You can't conceal it; it's what you become
Do you wonder, if there's more, more, more

CHORUS

What on earth…. are you on earth… for, are you on earth for
What on earth…. are you on earth… for, are you on earth for
What, now, why

BRIDGE

What is the man in the sky pointing you to do
What is your heart telling you
Are you listening, are you listening, are you listening, listening

CHORUS

What on earth…. are you on earth… for, are you on earth for
What on earth…. are you on earth… for, are you on earth for
What, now, why

"There From Here"

VERSE I

I've had my share of triumphs
Just enough to keep trying
I've had my share of upsets
But never one that I let

PRE-CHORUS

Never ever never let it keep me down,
Never ever never let it make me drown

CHORUS

Cause if we're going to get there from here
We have to change what we know
If we're going to get there from here
We have to be willing to grow
And set aside our troubles, set aside our fears
If we're going to get there from here

VERSE II

In every chance, lies an avenue
With every glance there's a reason to
With every doubt lies an answer
They burn on the road that swelters

PRE-CHORUS

But I never ever never let it steer me wrong
I never ever never let it keep me long

CHORUS

Cause if we're going to get there from here
We have to change what we know
If we're going to get there from here
We have to be willing to grow
And set aside our troubles, set aside our fears
If we're going to get there from here

BRIDGE

The inches turn into feet, and the feet become yards
Without knowing defeat, you never know who you really are
You never know who you really are, you never know who you really are.

CHORUS

Cause if we're going to get there from here
We have to change what we know
If we're going to get there from here
We have to be willing to grow
And set aside our troubles, set aside our fears
If we're going to get there from here

Copyright 2009 Brian David Music LLC

"Momentum"

VERSE I

The pace of the world won't stop
The race will never slow for the top
We're all trying to get there cause were all trying to get there

PRE-CHORUS

Just need some momentum behind me, A strong tailwind to find me
So I can put my foot down, and leave behind a dust cloud

CHORUS

Just need a little, need a little momentum
Just need a little, need a little momentum
Need the pendulum to swing my way
Need a strong desire that never fades
Just need a little, need a little momentum

VERSE II

The dreams of it all won't fade
The streams of fate will always find a way
While you're trying to get there, trying to get there
The goal of something more is real
No matter how much the world tries to steal
While you're trying to get there, you're trying to get there

CHORUS

Just need a little, need a little momentum

CHORUS

Not giving in, no I'm not giving in
Not giving in, no I'm not giving in
Cause I just need, a little momentum
Just need a little, need a little momentum

Copyright 2009 Brian David Music LLC

"The Road Ahead"

VERSE I

Behind the wheel of my life
I've tried to keep it between the lines
But in the vagueness of my goals
Lies questions beyond my control

PRE-CHORUS

In the distance are the answers
In the dust I've left my cancers, and
I'm leaving it all behind, I'm leaving it all behind

CHORUS

I can see the road ahead, visualize it in my head
I can see where I want to go. I was lost, but now I know

VERSE II

In the fragments of time
I've forgotten what I was trying to find
The past paths I have chosen
have managed to keep me frozen
And I can only respond, to what I think lies beyond
prepare for the best, in a future only I can invest

PRE-CHORUS

In the distance are the answers
In the dust I've left my cancers, and
I'm leaving it all behind, I'm leaving it all behind

CHORUS

I can see the road ahead, visualize it in my head
I can see where I want to go. I was lost, but now I know
I can see the road ahead, visualize it in my head
I can see where I want to go, I was lost, but now I know

BRIDGE

Something inside, is lingering, I'm finally doing, not just pretending
Something good, is not far away, in a dream of tomorrow, I see more
    than today
I see more than today

I can see the road ahead, visualize it in my head

I can see where I want to go. I was lost, but now I know, but now I know

"Energy"

VERSE I

It feels like I got one chance again

One last shot, one last stand

It seems like the world is in my hands

Cause I'm feeling the weight, feeling the weight again

CHORUS

I'm sinking my teeth in it, all my beliefs in it

The air that I breathe, along with all my energy

I'm sinking my teeth in it, all my beliefs in it

The air that I breathe, along with all my energy

VERSE II

And it feels like I've been right here before

I had it all, I was about to soar

Now I seem to have found a little something more

That I'm finding the meaning, finding the meaning for

CHORUS

I'm sinking my teeth in it, all my beliefs in it

The air that I breathe, along with all my energy

I'm sinking my teeth in it, all my beliefs in it

The air that I breathe, along with all my energy

BRIDGE

Is this all, is this all for me
Is this all, is this all for me
For me-------- for me-----
All that I got, all that I have, every ounce of all my energy
All that I got, all that I have, every ounce of all my energy
All that I got, all that I have, every ounce of all my energy
All that I got, all that I have, every ounce of all my energy

Copyright 2009 Brian David Music LLC

"Ten Steps Behind"

VERSE I

I don't know
If I'm ever gonna somehow catch
This world, I chase
on calculated bets
But there is one thing, I know
I know for sure
It's hard to catch up in this catch up world

CHORUS

And it feels like I am ten steps behind, all the time
and it feels like I am ten steps behind, all the time

VERSE II

I don't know
if I'm ever gonna cross the line
running from failures

on borrowed time
If there is one thing, I know
I know is inside
The closer I get, the harder I am going to fight

CHORUS

And it feels like I am ten steps behind, all the time
and it feels like I am ten steps behind, all the time
It feels like I'm running and running in place
It feels like I'm never the one being chased
With every step that I'm trying to take, I seem to find
I'm ten steps behind
Trying to catch up, from ten steps behind

CHORUS

And it feels like I am ten steps behind, all the time
and it feels like I am ten steps behind, all the time
It feels like I'm running and running in place
It feels like I'm never the one being chased
With every step that I'm trying to take, I seem to find
I'm ten steps behind
Trying to catch up, from ten steps behind

Copyright 2009 Brian David Music LLC

"Between the Lines"

VERSE I

I've been running on empty
on fumes and air
I've avoided the tempting

That leads to nowhere
I've been giving some thought
to the way things have been
Tried not to get caught
in the trap of always second guessing

CHORUS

And I------- been waiting for a moment
And I --------- been looking for a sign
And I ----------- been following my instincts
So I can find.. The answers hidden somewhere
Between the lines

VERSE II

I've been walking on eggshells
and least it feels that way
I've been listening to well
to thoughts I replay
I've been wanting some truth
to stare right in the eyes
To keep the part of my youth
From ever failing to try

CHORUS

And I------- been waiting for a moment
And I --------- been looking for a sign
And I ----------- been following my instincts
So I can find.. The answers hidden somewhere
Between the lines

"It's Not So Bad"

VERSE I

There seems to be, an endless theme
that's always there preventing me,
it keeps circling around, waiting for me to be down
But you're there now, so I don't drown

CHORUS

And every time I doubt today
that the good outweighs the bad
I just need you around, to shine the light on what we have
When I can't see clearly, I need you near me
When it's hard to realize, you look me in the eyes
And say… It's not so bad
No it's not so bad

VERSE II

Now you're here, to help me there
To shed the skin, I used to wear, and
Untie the knots, that keep twisting my thoughts
So I don't get caught not knowing what I've got

CHORUS

And every time I doubt today
that the good outweighs the bad
I just need you around, to shine the light on what we have
When I can't see clearly, I need you near me
When it's hard to realize, you look me in the eyes

And say... It's not so bad
No it's not so bad

BRIDGE

When it feels like I'm sinking
You keep me still thinking, It's not … so … bad, it's not so bad
When it's all overflowing, you keep me still knowing
It's not … so bad, it's not … so bad
No matter what, gets me down on my luck,
you need to say everything we'll be ok
No matter what, gets me down on my luck,
you just need to say everything we'll be ok

Copyright 2009 Brian David Music LLC

"Almost There"

VERSE I

Fighting the night and chasing the days
dreaming despite all the past in our way, all the past in our way
Watching the months and losing the years
Counting the stunts that got us both here, thru all the obstacles and fears

CHORUS

Oh we're almost there, it won't be long
To there from here, can't be any further now
We're almost there

VERSE II

Wrestling the thoughts and all the mistakes
Trying not to get caught in the days that feel safe, all the days that feel safe

Stuck in it all, as fears still accrue, hitting every wall, hoping we make it
   through, do everything we can do

CHORUS

Oh we're almost there, it won't be long
To there from here, can't be any further now
We're almost there
From where we are and where we'll be
It is not that far for you and me

BRIDGE

As hard as it gets and trying the times
There is one thing I keep close in my mind, and it's you.

CHORUS

Oh we're almost there, it won't be long
To there from here, can't be any further now
We're almost there
We're almost, we're almost, we're almost there
We're almost, we're almost, we're almost there

Copyright 2009 Brian David Music LLC

"Always Wondering"

VERSE I

I'm always wondering, if the life is what it seems
I'm always wondering, if the past is just a dream
I'm always wondering, if the path I'm on is right
I'm always wondering, if the answers

Will shed some light, shed some light ----
So I'm not always wondering

VERSE II

I'm always wondering, if all history is relevant
I'm always wondering, if success will be permanent
I'm always wondering, if purpose can be found
I'm always wondering, if my thoughts will
Keep weighing me down, keep weighting me down

CHORUS

What can I do, what can I say
To change the world just for a day
Where is the truth, what's here to stay
Will I find the signs, that show the way
So I'm not
I'm not, always wondering

VERSE III

I'm always wondering, what the future will entail
I'm always wondering, if love will prevail
I'm always wondering, if there something left to find
I'm always wondering, if I'm wasting
My precious time, my precious time

CHORUS

What can I do, what can I say
To change the world just for a day
Where is the truth, what's here to stay
Will I find the signs, that show the way

So I'm not
I'm not always wondering

"The Next Mile"

VERSE I

Down the path of least resistance
in a sea of green lights
Lies another left turn that should have been right
Deep in the distance
lies an all of your dreams
Past the virtues of patience and faint memories

PRE-CHORUS

When you're feeling like you're getting nowhere
And you're breathing in the wrong kind of air
Take one last breath, one last rest
and take that next step

CHORUS

To the next mile, to the next mile
To the next mile, to the next mile
Just pretend that you're blind to the obstacles that you find
And keep fighting your way thru time
To the next mile

VERSE II

In the shadows they hide
all the voices that tempt you

trying to keep you behind in the dark of the blue
In the glimmers of hope
There's room to believe
Past excuses you've made into a great big sea

PRE-CHORUS

When you're feeling like you're getting nowhere
And you're breathing in the wrong kind of air
Take one last breath, one last rest
and take that next step

CHORUS

To the next mile, to the next mile
To the next mile, to the next mile
Just pretend that you're blind to the obstacles that you find
And keep fighting your way thru time
To the next mile

BRIDGE

Today is worth ten tomorrows
Today is worth ten tomorrows
Today is worth ten tomorrows
So make today worthwhile, on your way to the next mile
To the next mile, to the next mile

Copyright 2009 Brian David Music LLC

APPENDIX 5

FAVORITE INSPIRATIONAL QUOTES

"The way to get started is to quit talking and begin doing."
— Walt Disney

"Your success in life will be in direct proportion to what you do after you've done the things you're expected to do."
— Brian Tracy

"The one thing that can never be taken away from a person is their freedom to choose their response to any given set of circumstances."
"When you repeatedly see yourself achieving a goal in your minds eye, you will consciously begin to believe that you can achieve it."
— Brian Tracy

"Each moment of our life, we either invoke or destroy our dreams."

– Jim Rohn

"Without a future well-defined, we take hesitant steps."

– Jim Rohn

"If we are vague with the plan for our life, we will end up with vague results."

– Jim Rohn

"If you had negative thoughts yesterday, you'll have those same negative thoughts today and tomorrow unless you do something about it."

– John Maxwell

"The story we tell ourselves and the attitude we have because of that story will determine how things go for us in life."

– Jim Rohn

"The problem is that we want change, but we don't want to put the work in to get the change we desire."
"The problem is we want more, but don't act like we want more on a daily basis."
"Our actions speak volumes as they say. Our actions tell the story of how badly we want something."

– Jim Rohn

"Success is not what we get, but who we become."

– Jim Rohn

"You first need to understand why you are where you are now before you can understand and know how you can get to where you deserve to be."

– Jim Rohn

"If you argue for your limitations you're going to get your limitations."

– Richard Bach

"Some people live 90 years. Some people live one year 90 times. They don't explore and expand their horizon."

– Mary Morrissey

"Self-discipline is this: getting yourself to do something, even though you don't feel like it, because the reward for getting it done far exceeds the temporary unpleasantness of the task itself."

– attributed to Elbert Hubbard

"People cling to an unsatisfactory way of life rather than change to get something better for fear of getting something worse."

– Eric Hoffer

"We don't always get what we want, we get what we choose."

– Jim Rohn

"Failure is not a single cataclysmic event. You don't feel overnight. Instead, failure is a few errors in judgment repeated every day."

– Jim Rohn

"If your past doesn't define you, what does? What defines you, is what you do NOW!"

– Jim Rohn

"Your future is created by what you do today, not tomorrow, and the best way to predict your future is by creating it."

– Jim Rohn

"Whatever we focus our energy on, we get more of it."

– Tony Robbins

"If you want to know what your future holds, look to your actions; the other best predictor of your future."

– Jim Rohn

"The greatest gift you can give someone is your full attention."

– Jim Rohn

"Learn to appreciate what you have, before time forces you to appreciate what you had."

– Ziad K. Abdelnour

"Life was designed not to give us what we need, but to give us what we deserve."

– Jim Rohn

ACKNOWLEDGMENTS

Writing a book has been a goal of mine for over 15 years. I owe this goal becoming a reality to a neighborhood friend named Art Howard, who I ran into at Jerry's in Woodbury in the summer of 2024. He happened to work at Wiley and forwarded my intro and table of contents to the right people.

To my friend Shawn Carlin, who has been a student of personal growth and self-development and a constant friend in my life. He has been not only a friend but a mentor and sometimes a therapist.

To my friend Doug Andersen, who has been there every step of the way with deep conversations and insightful advice.

To my parents, who believed in me and supported my dreams and passions.

To my kids, who have shown me the meaning of life and made me want to be the best father I can be.

To my fiancé, Sarah, who has supported me and loved me at my worst. Her patience and encouragement when I lost belief in myself will always be something I am extremely grateful for.

To my brother Chad, who has authored many novellas and books, and who inspired me to write on a topic I am passionate about.

A special thanks to the whole team at Wiley for giving me direction and advice to make this book the best it can be.

I also want to acknowledge the contribution of all the people I have come in contact with who have inspired me and encouraged me through the years.

Lastly, thank you, the reader, for taking the time to read this book to improve your life. I hope the ideas and insight have given you a new perspective and inspired you to create a life going forward that is richer with more meaning, accomplishments, experiences, and making a difference.

ABOUT THE AUTHOR

Brian David Muller is a seasoned financial advisor whose expertise spans over two decades of helping people achieve financial independence. He is the founder of Momentous Wealth Advisors in Woodbury, Minnesota, and a certified Health and Life Coach through the Health Coach Institute.

Beyond his professional credentials, Brian's journey as a musician adds a unique depth to his perspective on life. When not spending time with his family, traveling, or advising clients, Brian spends his time creating music. Since 2006, he has released three albums with the Brian David Band and eight singles as a solo artist. His song "Ladder To The Sky," inspired by his son's dream, has helped raise funds for grief support programs, and he hopes to continue to use music to raise money for causes he is passionate about.

His weekly podcast, "Wealth Decisions by Brian," reaches thousands of listeners with practical insights on building richer lives through mindset development and smart decisions around money.

In 2017, following the loss of his wife, Air Force Veteran Amie Muller, Brian channeled his grief into purpose by establishing the Amie Muller Foundation to support veterans with a cancer diagnosis who were exposed to toxic burn pits during service in Iraq or Afghanistan.

Brian brings unique insight to personal growth through his experiences in finance, health, creativity, and resilience. Having immersed himself in over 200 personal growth books, he distills complex concepts into actionable wisdom that readers can apply to live healthier, wealthier, and more fulfilling lives.

INDEX